Imperative Narratives

Imperative Narratives

Storytelling Secrets for Teachers, Staff, and Administrators

Mike Tveten

ROWMAN & LITTLEFIELD
Lanham • Boulder • New York • London

Published by Rowman & Littlefield
An imprint of The Rowman & Littlefield Publishing Group, Inc.
4501 Forbes Boulevard, Suite 200, Lanham, Maryland 20706
www.rowman.com

6 Tinworth Street, London SE11 5AL

Copyright © 2019 by Mike Tveten

All rights reserved. No part of this book may be reproduced in any form or by any electronic or mechanical means, including information storage and retrieval systems, without written permission from the publisher, except by a reviewer who may quote passages in a review.

British Library Cataloguing in Publication Information Available

Library of Congress Cataloging-in-Publication Data Available

ISBN: 978-1-4758-5081-9 (cloth)
ISBN: 978-1-4758-5082-6 (pbk.)
ISBN: 978-1-4758-5083-3 (electronic)

To my wife and best friend, Lisa Holtorf, for all her love and support. Also, to my stepson Brett Champlin and his partner Jessica, and to my daughter Amanda Tveten and her partner Chance, thanks for all your love and support as well. Thanks also to my mom, Gloria Tveten, and to the memory of my dad, John Tveten—you are both published authors, and pointed me in the right direction since day one.

Contents

Foreword: Little Stories about a Great Topic *Clyde Freeman Herreid*	ix
Foreword *David R. Katz III*	xi
Preface	xiii
Acknowledgments	xvii
Introduction	1
1 The Power of Storytelling in Education	5
2 We Are Wired for Story	9
3 What Makes a Story Compelling?	13
4 Choosing Stories to Tell	23
5 How to Tell Stories in Any Educational Setting	31
6 Weaving Stories Into Lectures, Discussions, and Activities	39
7 Digital Stories and Video Stories	47
8 Photographs That Tell Stories	53
9 Empowering Students to Tell Their Own Stories	61
10 Storytelling for Staff and Administrators	69
11 Changing the Narrative to Make a Difference	77
Appendix: Examples of Stories Written by Students	85
References	109

About the Author 113

Foreword

Little Stories about a Great Topic

Clyde Freeman Herreid

When I was five, I had a great blue book that I treasured. Inside there were adventures and discoveries—not about dragons, princesses, knights, or magicians but about the actual, physical world—places that I longed to see if only to make sure they really did exist. Giant sequoia trees so big that cars could drive through tunnels carved in their trunks. A Niagara River that poured millions of gallons of water over cliffs to the rocks below and killed people who tried to travel over those cliffs in barrels. A Grand Canyon that, revered by Native Americans, was millions of years old with mysterious fossils found imprinted on its stones. A Mammoth Cave filled with towering stalagmites and stalactites and walls of crystals that glittered like diamonds. The great Panama Canal. Yellowstone National Park. New York City. The Great Lakes. And . . . and . . . and . . . oh, I loved that book, *Little Stories of a Great Country*, by Laura Antoinette.

I think of it now as I read over the pages of narrative that flow from the pen of our tour guide, Mike Tveten, of Pima Community College. In a few pages, he has captured the basic magic of the case study method and its ability to engage the listener like no other approach because it taps into the basic biochemistry/psychology of the brain and its need to make sense of the world. Tveten divides his journey into short, straightforward chapters that display the big picture of the case method: why we are wired to appreciate stories; what makes them compelling; which stories to choose and how to weave them into lectures, discussions, and activities; how cases can be developed out of photographs, digital files, and videos; and . . . and . . . and . . .

The author even lets the students in on the fun, empowering them to write their own narratives. His egalitarian approach does not stop there; he lets staff and administrators tag along on the journey with their own particular vantage points. Finally, he lets us in on some self-help lessons as he winds up encouraging readers to change their life narratives if they are so inclined. This may be a little book, but it has a big vision: to change the way we teach and lead our lives—academically and beyond.

Clyde Freeman Herreid
University at Buffalo
SUNY Distinguished Teaching Professor
Director of the National Center for Case Study Teaching in Science

Foreword

David R. Katz III

Mike Tveten and I first crossed paths when I was delivering a keynote presentation at his place of employment, Pima Community College, in Tucson, Arizona. This was during the summer of 2015, so it was kinda hot—like 108 degrees in the shade hot!

The first "story" I told my audience of 400 folks at that college was of my initial drive in the great state of Arizona. I noticed in amazement as I crossed bridge after bridge on the interstate that there were signs by the bridges that named the creek or stream I was crossing. The thing was . . . there was no actual water of any kind in the named creek! I explained to them (tongue in cheek) that where I come from, at the foothills of the Adirondack Mountains in the Mohawk Valley of central New York, we always make sure to put plenty of water in our named creeks and lakes. That got me a good laugh and marked me as an intrepid, mixed-up adventurer and storyteller making my first sojourn into their desert world!

That short story also did exactly what Mike, a seasoned college educator, says stories will do, in this book on "storytelling secrets." It engaged the audience emotionally in my presentation by arousing their actual feelings associated with their parched environment, which is marked by extreme heat and very, very little water. Did I mention there was actually no water?! The emotional and sensory parts of their brains were aroused, and they were then in a far better position to absorb and retain the information that followed, which dealt with the topic of emotional intelligence and establishing empowering emotional connections with others.

What a remarkable coincidence that my topic connected with Mike's passion for reaching people by connecting to them emotionally through the use of stories! This is what stories can do for us all as we try to reach others with important information that we hope will enrich their existence and empower them. Stories have humor, pathos, inspiration, confusion, triumph, and all those wonderful feelings that are so exquisitely bound up within all of our lives. As educators and leaders, we learn that when our important information gets wrapped in a story, it makes the concept come alive to our human brains, which have evolved and are enveloped in our very real, objective, sensory-based world. To our audience, the story becomes bona fide proof of an idea's existence and efficacy in the real world.

I returned to Mike's college the following year to continue my work, and then, like a bad penny, I turned up again at a national conference on higher education that Mike was attending in San Francisco. He attended my presentation on presentations titled . . . wait for it . . . "Compelling Communication!" In that particular learning experience/show, I spent a lot of time breaking down and demonstrating the significance and anatomy of storytelling. Needless to say, I was preaching to the choir with Mike in the audience. From that point on, our professional friendship was cemented.

My favorite part of Mike's work, besides the fact that he is letting me stick my two cents in with this foreword, is that he breaks down the necessity for tapping into storytelling to positively affect learning and does so in a manner that makes it all seem accessible and doable to practitioners like us. His assertion "Everyone can be a great storyteller" is supported by painstakingly providing us with a very practical step-by-step guide to developing the necessary skills. He makes sure we know that this is not only for naturally outgoing, theatrically inclined, aspiring thespians. His resounding message, that we regular folk can get really good at this stuff with practice, is both hopeful and encouraging.

The kicker in all this is that telling stories is flat-out fun for you and for your audience. That kind of fun opens people up to connection, collaboration, and creative thinking, and it makes them want to come back for more. The bottom line is that learning and empowerment are improved. Mike says that "the goal of this book is to help anyone in education apply these three rules [of storytelling] in order to make a difference in the world." My hope is that we all read this book and then go tell our story in our own unique voice, and that we all make a difference in the places and spaces we reside in, with the people we are privileged to teach and lead! Peace.

Professor David R. Katz III
davidkatzpresents.com

Preface

There are three important rules about stories and storytelling that everyone should know:

1. *Our brains are wired for story.* We crave stories, and we can't get enough of them. Stories aren't just for kids—people of all ages listen to, tell, love, and cherish stories.
2. *Storytelling is the single most powerful tool for teaching anything to anyone.* People have been learning through stories since the dawn of human civilization. Tying a concept to a memorable story is the best method to ensure students will never forget the importance and relevance of the concept.
3. *Changing your story can change your life.* The stories we tell are even more powerful than the "power of positive thinking." Changing our own story from one of negativity to something more positive can help bring about a positive change in ourselves. Changing the stories we tell about other people can change their lives and ours, creating opportunities for success, a more meaningful and productive workplace, and a better future for everyone.

The goal of this book is to help anyone in education apply these three rules in order to make a difference in the world. For whom is this book written? This book is for you (!) if

- you are a classroom teacher who teaches any age level from early childhood to adults,
- you are a staff member or an administrator at any type of educational institution,

- you are a coach, a mentor, or a tutor,
- you are in a classroom, a lab, or a museum; in the field; or on a job site; or,
- in any manner, you help learners learn or teachers teach.

Tying any concept to a story is the best way to teach any concept, and the most effective teachers weave stories into everything they teach. But the importance of the narrative goes well beyond how your learners learn or how you teach. Changing the stories you tell can turn your school around, turn your students' lives around, and even turn your own life around. This book can help you

- change the stories you tell about yourself,
- change the stories you tell about your students,
- change the stories your students tell about themselves,
- change the stories you tell about your school, and
- change the stories that others tell about your school.

Nothing can describe the importance of story like a story can. Here are a few of my personal stories that illustrate the power of changing the narrative. I have been teaching biology at Pima Community College in Tucson, Arizona, for many years, having started part-time in 1988 and then becoming full-time in 1992. After several years of teaching, I knew I needed to find new and better ways to create more meaningful learning experiences for my students.

In January 2005, I participated in a week-long workshop given by Dr. Clyde "Kipp" Herreid, who is world-renowned for his case study approach to teaching. About halfway through the workshop, when I was feeling very frustrated, I went to Kipp and said, "This approach only works if you are a great storyteller! And I am not a storyteller!" Kipp looked at me, and with his grandfatherly smile and a twinkle in his eye, he said, "Ah . . . but you *could* be!"

It took a few weeks for that comment to really sink in. But once it did, I began incorporating stories into my teaching. I started simply at first, repeating some of the engaging stories from the history of biology. Next, I expanded my list of stories to include biology-related items from the news, and stories involving celebrities with whom my students could identify. Eventually, I began sharing my own experiences as personal stories. I quickly felt that I was becoming a much more effective teacher.

A year later, I collected some empirical evidence to support my use of stories. I had been unhappy with the textbook I was using for my one-semester general biology for nonmajors course, so I switched textbooks in January in preparation for the spring semester. By March, I was a little disappointed that I did not see much of a change in the performance of the students. So I gave my students an anonymous survey just before spring break, asking questions like "What do you think of the textbook?" and "What areas of the subject matter do you find interesting?"

The results floored me. Regarding the textbook, I received answers that included, "It's heavy," "It has a pretty cover," and "I don't know, because it has been in the trunk of my car all semester." When asked about the areas of biology they found interesting, students told me they were the same areas that I had told stories about in class.

I then spent the week of spring break totally immersed in a new project, completely overhauling the entire course into one that was topic-based and full of stories as opposed to the traditional, chapter-based approach that followed the textbook. When students showed up to class on Monday after spring break, there was a big surprise awaiting them! At first they weren't sure about the idea—they said they were comfortable with how my class had been running. But they sensed my excitement and said they were willing to try the new format.

For the rest of the semester, we approached each area with a relevant topic, like diabetes and heart disease, and I introduced each topic with a story. It turned out to be the ideal teaching experiment. I had one group of 26 students with three exam scores before spring break and another three exam scores after the change at spring break, plus attendance records. The results were even better than I had hoped. Exam scores improved by over 10% (a full letter grade!), and attendance improved by nearly 20%. I have since continued to make stories the core of my teaching.

Changing the narrative can also make a difference for your school. In August 2014, I began a 16-month stint as an acting academic dean. The college had been through some difficult times in the previous couple of years, and the stories being told about the college in the local newspaper were not always favorable. While I was dean, I did my best to change the stories we told about our students and our college. Here are three examples from my time in administration:

- In the spring semester of 2015, I had a student in her early 40s who worked incredibly hard in my evening biology class. She earned an A despite working full time, dealing with an impending divorce, and raising a kid in high school and two kids in elementary school. What was her motivation for working so hard? She was determined to graduate and walk across the stage together with her 21-year-old daughter, who was also graduating. At the All College Day event at the start of the following fall semester, I arranged for her to attend, and her inspirational success story was shared with the entire college.
- A few years ago, I had a student in my beginning biology course for allied health who (like many of my students) was young, lacked focus, and had poor study skills. She continually made an effort to improve and just

barely passed the class, thanks to a lot of tutoring and encouragement on my part. A few years later, while I was dean, she stopped by the campus to tell me that she was now working as a lead nurse in the heart transplant ward at a prestigious hospital. She had gone from being a C student to the top of her field. I shared her success story with faculty across the college, reminding teachers that not just some but all of our students have the potential and the ability to accomplish great things if we provide a bit of nurturing, guidance, and encouragement.
- When I heard there was a possibility for our campus to host a regional STEM Adventure event for over 1,000 fourth through eighth graders, I jumped at the opportunity. It turned out to be a highly successful event that got citywide media publicity for all the right reasons, plus we put the idea of one day coming to our community college into the heads of over 1,000 kids. This has now become an annual event at our campus, and it has nationwide recognition.

Of course, I can't take sole credit for changing the narrative at our college, but I know I made a difference by helping to change the stories we were telling about our school and our students.

Many best-selling books have been written about the power of story and the effectiveness of using story to bring about change. These books have targeted novelists, writers for TV and movies, marketing executives, CEOs of for-profit and nonprofit companies large and small, and even politicians.

But I believe this book is the first of its kind written just for teachers, staff, and administrators in education. I honestly can't think of an area where change, and the changing of the narrative, is more important than in education. I want to help you become a great storyteller so that you personally can bring about change—for yourself, for your students, and for your school.

Acknowledgments

To Clyde Herreid, thanks for getting me starting in storytelling. To Eric Jensen, thanks for helping me develop a plan for sharing storytelling with educators. To Sandra Paulick and Tim Kelliher, thanks for being so supportive of this project during a great summer in Montana. And Sandra, thanks so much for the editing and proofreading.

I also want to thank so many of my peers at Pima Community College—in particular, thanks to Tom Jordan, Jennifer Katcher, Randy Munsen, Chuck Becker, Emily Halvorson, Susan Kramer, and Parrish Watson for all the great ideas and for swapping stories for so many years. Thanks to Clyde Herreid and David Katz for writing forewords, and to Eric Jensen, Molly McCloy, Kelly Hogan, Dolores Duran-Cerda, and Ike Shibley for the kind words. Thank you to the folks at Rowman & Littlefield, including Helen Subbio, Jo-Ann Parks, Emily Tuttle, Carlie Wall, Hannah Fisher (and everyone else at R&L who is helping me!), with special thanks to Tom Koerner for believing in this project from the beginning. Finally, thanks to all my students over the last 30 years, especially those who contributed a story for the appendix of this book as well as those who are the subjects of the stories throughout the book. In particular, I want to thank John for allowing me to publish Pat's story here—Pat was a beautiful soul, and she will be missed.

Introduction

Would you like to be a more effective teacher?
Would you like to be a more effective administrator?
Would you like to be a more effective staff member at your school?
Would you like to see your students be more successful?
Would you like to see your school shine in a better light?
Would you like to be happier in your job?

If your answer to any of these questions is "yes," then this book is for you. The easiest way to achieve all of these goals is through storytelling. Start reading this book today, start implementing these ideas today, and you will see the benefits immediately. Just pick a chapter and dive in!

Chapter 1, "The Power of Storytelling in Education," gives some examples of how storytelling can help improve student learning by tying stories to content, and shows the benefits of changing the stories that teachers tell about themselves and their students. There are also examples of how changing the narratives of our schools can help students be more successful and can change the way the community views its local schools.

Chapter 2, "We Are Wired for Story," cites the neuroscience research that shows the impact of storytelling on the human brain. This chapter also gives you a homework assignment: to count the number of times that you hear the terms *story* and *narrative* in your daily life.

Chapter 3, "What Makes a Story Compelling?" outlines 12 fundamental storytelling truths. Follow these guidelines, and you can quickly become a great storyteller in any setting.

Chapter 4, "Choosing Stories to Tell," presents ideas on how to find the right story for every situation. The stories you tell can be based on historical or current events, or you can tell your own personal stories.

Chapter 5, "How to Tell Stories in Any Educational Setting," presents some ideas on incorporating storytelling in situations from a traditional classroom to a hybrid or flipped classroom to an online course and to other nontraditional educational settings.

Chapter 6, "Weaving Stories into Lectures, Discussions, and Activities," gives ideas on how to find stories for case studies and how to use stories to improve critical thinking.

Chapter 7, "Digital Stories and Video Stories," describes the variety of methods for effective digital storytelling. With the increase in online instruction and the use of social media, digital storytelling is critically important to being able to change and share your narrative.

Chapter 8 is titled "Photographs That Tell Stories." Originally, paintings were used to tell stories, but the development of photography allowed people to capture scenes and events that were far more accurate in telling stories that are true. You can use photographs to start discussions, to introduce topics, or to make oral or written stories more powerful.

Chapter 9, "Empowering Students to Tell Their Own Stories," shows that students can demonstrate critical thinking by relating their own stories to content in your course. You will find that when students share their stories with you and with other students, people become more connected and conversations improve. Students who have experienced challenges and trauma and are dealing with their struggles can also find that telling their personal stories is therapeutic.

Chapter 10, "Storytelling for Staff and Administrators," is written especially for readers who do more than just teach. You can learn to change the internal stories that employees tell about your school, improving the organizational climate in the workplace. Changing the internal stories is the first step in changing the external stories about your school that are shared with the community. Once the narratives of your school become more positive, the entire community will better understand your school's mission and values.

Chapter 11, "Changing the Narrative to Make a Difference," addresses what are perhaps the most important stories to change—the stories you tell about yourself. These are also the hardest stories to change. This is much more than just the power of positive thinking—this is about taking a hard look at yourself and your situation and rewriting the stories in your head that you tell yourself and others. Changing your own narrative can change your outlook on life and make you much happier and more effective in your job.

In the appendix, you will find several stories written by students that demonstrate the importance of enabling students to tell their own stories.

Some of these stories will shock you with their descriptions of the challenges that these students have faced. Starting to listen to the stories your students want to tell will change you in a very positive way.

Just pick a chapter and start reading. Perhaps start late in the book and then go back to chapter 3 to learn the 12 fundamental truths of effective storytelling. Take a look at chapter 4 about how to gather the stories you want to tell. Shed a few tears while reading the student stories in the appendix. Be sure to read chapter 11 and take a hard look at the stories you tell about yourself. Being a great storyteller is the best way to be a more effective teacher, administrator, or staff member. Learning to change the narrative can save your school, your students, and even yourself.

Chapter One

The Power of Storytelling in Education

Teaching with a story is the most powerful tool that we can use as teachers. And changing the stories we tell about ourselves, about our schools, and about our students can literally change lives. Nowhere are stories more important than in education.

Teachers can be more effective in helping students learn when teachers tell stories. Tie any concept to a memorable story, and students never forget the concept.

For example, in a general biology class, one of the topics covered in genetics is autosomal dominant inheritance. To put the topic in context, a teacher can share the story of Nancy Wexler, whose mom died of Huntington's Disease. Nancy, with a 50% chance of inheriting the disease from her mother, was determined to help other families facing the disease, so she became a genetics researcher. After studying the genetics of a community near Lake Maracaibo in Venezuela, she located the gene that causes Huntington's.

Nancy developed the test for the gene but did not take the test herself; just knowing she had a 50% chance of inheriting Huntington's was scary enough, and she didn't want a positive test result to determine the direction of her life. Nancy's sister, Alice, also had a 50% chance of inheriting the disease, but Alice did want to know her future.

In fact, Alice was the first person to take the genetic test that Nancy had developed. A negative result for Alice, plus the fact that Nancy is now in her 70s and still healthy, shows that neither daughter inherited the autosomal dominant gene from their mother (Wexler, 1996). While students may forget the details of inheritance in a typical biology class, students remember this concept because they remember Nancy's story.

Teachers can change their own stories. These include the stories they tell others about themselves as teachers and the stories they tell themselves about their own teaching. Changing their story can help teachers improve their skills, avoid burnout, and change the direction of their teaching.

Emily Smith is a fifth-grade English language arts teacher in Austin, Texas. Emily recently shared how she changed her own story. She used to describe herself as a great teacher, helping her students become great writers. But one day, a young male student bluntly told her that "she couldn't understand because she was a white lady" (Strauss, 2015).

Emily knew he was right. After a good cry, she set about changing her curriculum, bringing in literature, documents, videos, discussions, and images that better reflected her students' ethnic and cultural backgrounds and that better engaged her students. She described this journey in her acceptance speech for the 2015 Donald H. Graves Award for Excellence in the Teaching of Writing (Strauss, 2015). Emily changed her story and in doing so changed the direction of her own life and the lives of her students.

Teachers can change the stories of their students, including both the stories that the teachers tell about their students and the stories that students tell about themselves. Students who may be statistically destined for failure can become successful when their stories change.

Olly Neal describes himself as having been "a poor black kid with an attitude." He lived in a house with no electricity along with 12 siblings and a father who had a second-grade education. Olly was a regular shoplifter, including at the jobs where he worked part-time in high school, and his future was not particularly bright.

Olly was the first student to make English teacher Mildred Grady cry. At the start of his senior year in high school, he cut a class and went to the library. Ms. Grady had just set up a display of books in the library, and from a distance she watched Olly pick up a novel with a picture of a sexy woman on the cover—and steal it. Naturally, Ms. Grady was angry at first. But rather than report him, Ms. Grady hoped that Olly would enjoy reading the book, so she went out and bought another book by the same author and put it on display.

Sure enough, Olly read the book, sneaked it back into the library, found the book Ms. Grady had planted for him, and stole that one. This continued, with Ms. Grady secretly finding new books specifically for Olly, and Olly secretly borrowing and returning them. After reading several novels, he began branching out in his reading, seeking harder books and even beginning to read the newspaper and magazines. After high school, he went to college and then law school, was appointed the first black district prosecuting attorney in Arkansas, and eventually became an appellate court judge.

Years later, at a high school reunion, Ms. Grady, with tears in her eyes, confided to Olly that she had watched him steal that first book. She understood his embarrassment at being seen checking out a book, and she had driven 70 miles to find more novels by the same author, paying for them out of her own pocket. Mildred Grady changed the story of her student and changed his life. Her impact was even felt in the next generation, when Olly's daughter, Karama, earned a doctorate in genetics, taught bioethics at Emory University, and now runs a community development program in Arkansas (Kristof, 2012).

Teachers can help change the stories of their schools and districts, bringing about a change in school climate. In today's world, where so many schools are labeled as "underperforming," the fastest way to turn things around is for teachers, staff, and administrators to change the stories they tell themselves and the community about their school.

In describing school culture, Peterson and Deal (1998) portrayed schools with strong, positive cultures as "schools where the informal network of storytellers, heroes, and heroines provides a social web of information, support, and history." Peterson (2002) further describes how teachers, staff, and administrators can nurture the school culture's positive aspects by telling stories of accomplishment and collaboration whenever there's an opportunity.

Educators at two schools in Virginia successfully changed the stories they told of their schools. Both Dudley and Windy Gap Elementary Schools in Franklin County, Virginia, implemented the Success for All program ("Success Stories," 2015). Although the decision to implement the program was made by school administration, it would never have been successful without buy-in from the teachers.

Regular assemblies at both schools highlight successes by individual students, by classrooms, and by grades. Both schools share student success stories with parents and the wider community and recognize the parents and community members who have helped. Within a year of implementation, the number of Dudley students reading on or above grade level increased from 58% to 80%, and the state's Standard of Learning (SOL) scores went from an 86% pass rate to a 92% pass rate.

At Windy Gap, the increase in reading scores was even more dramatic, rising from 46% to 82%. By changing the climate and focusing on stories of cooperative learning, collaboration, encouragement, achievement, and family and community involvement, the teachers helped change the stories at their schools, the stories of their students, and even their own stories as teachers.

In this book, we will discuss the characteristics of effective stories and then look at available tools and the methods of implementing these tools for changing narratives and teaching with stories, with the goal of helping you change your own story and those of your students and your school.

KEY POINTS FROM CHAPTER 1

- Student learning improves when teachers tell stories. Tie any concept to a memorable story, and students never forget the concept.
- Teachers can change their own stories. Changing the narrative helps teachers improve their skills, avoid burnout, and change the direction of their teaching.
- Teachers can help change the stories of their students. Students who may be statistically destined for failure can become successful when their stories change.
- Teachers can help change the stories of their schools and districts, bringing about a change in school climate. The fastest way to turn things around for an underperforming school is for teachers, staff, and administrators to change the stories they tell themselves and the community about their school.

Chapter Two

We Are Wired for Story

The field of neuroscience explains the importance of stories in initiating brain activity. Researchers have long known that when a person is presented with facts and written information, only the language regions of the brain, namely, Broca's area and Wernicke's area, are activated.

In contrast, when people are encountering intense stimuli from their eyes, ears, nose, taste, and touch, multiple brain regions are activated, including the sensory cortex, motor cortex, olfactory cortex, visual cortex, auditory cortex, and cerebellum. These areas literally light up on the computer screen when using functional magnetic resonance imaging (fMRI) to scan for brain activity.

It turns out that simply reading or hearing a story that describes these stimuli can also activate multiple brain regions in the same way. In 2006, researchers in Spain discovered that when participants read words related to smell, the olfactory cortex was activated, just as an actual fragrance would do (González et al., 2006).

Lacey, Stilla, and Sathian (2012) showed a similar response—activation of the sensory cortex—when participants read metaphors involving texture. Mar (2011) looked at a total of 86 fMRI studies, concluding there was a substantial overlap in the brain networks used to process information from stories and the brain networks used to process information from interactions with other individuals and the real world. We are quite literally "wired for story."

This activation of the brain by stories occurs right down at the molecular level. For more than a decade, Dr. Paul Zak, a neuroscientist (and economist) at Claremont Graduate University, has been studying the link between the production in the brain of the neuropeptide oxytocin and various emotions and behaviors, such as empathy, kindness, generosity, trust, and cooperation.

There are numerous interactions between people that can lead to the endogenous release of oxytocin, increasing the positive effects on emotion and behavior. To test the power of story, Zak (2014, 2015) has shown that even video or audio inputs of character-driven stories with emotional content can also lead to the release of oxytocin as well as to the same positive effects on emotion.

This explains why everyone craves stories. This explains why people read novels, why they go to the movies, and why they watch sitcoms and reality TV. This explains why storytelling is the oldest form of teaching and learning. This explains why a concept tied to a story is retained by a student much longer than a concept that is not tied to a story. This explains why the stories that educators tell about themselves, about their students, and about their schools have such a profound impact on their future.

Here is a challenge for you—an assignment for you to complete over the next few days. Listen to everything in your environment (everything from discussions at work, discussions with friends and family, and what you see, hear, and read in the media), and make a mental note every time you hear the term *story*.

Try to keep count of the number of times you hear the word. You can even keep a little notebook handy and make tick marks every time you hear it. If you are keeping a written record, you can even keep a list of how the term *story* is used, such as news story, human interest story, politicians spinning the story, the back story, or the origin story.

You will also hear the term *narrative*, which is essentially just another term for *story*. Some people prefer the term *narrative* to *story*, particularly in academia, in literature, and sometimes in marketing. (In coming up with a title for this book, the hope was that the phrase *Imperative Narratives* might catch people's attention and pique their curiosity a little more than a book about "stories.")

While listening for the word *story*, think about how your own life is enriched by stories. Do you enjoy movies or TV shows, and if so, how much of your enjoyment is tied to the stories of the main characters? Perhaps you watch sports. Do you get wrapped up in the stories of victory and defeat that challenge individual athletes and their teams?

If you watch TV, which commercials stick in your head? Are they the commercials that tell a story? Do you prefer reading fiction or nonfiction? Most people associate fiction with stories, but even nonfiction is filled with stories that can catch and hold your attention.

Even the photographs and artwork encountered every day, whether the images bring you joy or make you turn away, often tell a story. Sometimes an image can lead you to create a story in your head. Sometimes the story told in a photo is so blatantly obvious and so compelling that the photo can bring about a wave of compassion or a call to arms to an entire nation or even to all of humanity.

No matter your age, certain historical images that everyone has seen are fixed in your mind, such as the image of young John F. Kennedy Jr. saluting as his father's horse-drawn hearse rolls by, or the image of a young girl screaming as she runs naked down the street of her village in Vietnam after being burned by napalm. Even a photo of a polar bear can be more than just a photo of a polar bear when that bear is precariously perched on a tiny block of Arctic ice melting on a warming planet.

Stories are powerful. Everyone wants them, enjoys them, craves them, and are called to action by them. It would be easy to write an entire book just about the power of story, but those books have already been written. The hope is that if you just listen and count the number of times you hear the words *story* and *narrative* being used, and think about the impact of stories in your own life, you will be completely on board about the importance and the power of story. You will be ready to jump right into chapter 3 and look at what makes a story compelling.

KEY POINTS FROM CHAPTER 2

- Reading or hearing a story about an event can activate multiple brain regions in the same way as actually experiencing the event. The human brain is literally wired for story.
- You encounter stories every day during conversations, while reading, while watching TV, and through social media. Your homework assignment is to listen for the words *story* and *narrative* in these venues, and think about the impact of stories on your life.

Chapter Three

What Makes a Story Compelling?

Many books have been written about stories and storytelling, with "rules" for telling stories and details on the various categories of stories, how they are composed, how to diagram a story arc, and so forth. But for this book, let's keep it simple. After all, the goal is to have you telling stories right away!

The most important facts to remember when telling a story is that great stories are

- resonant,
- compelling,
- impactful, and
- memorable.

If you are trying to help students learn by tying a story to a concept, then, in particular, make sure your story is memorable.

If you decide to change your own story, shape it into the most compelling and impactful story possible. If you help change the story of a student, make sure the new story is meaningful and memorable. If you help change the story of your school, make it a compelling story that has a positive impact on the entire community.

There are no rules or instructions that must under all circumstances be followed when telling a story—everyone has their own style. But there are some fundamental truths about great stories and storytelling that all storytellers should keep in mind when they are crafting a compelling and impactful story that resonates with the audience.

Randy Olson, Dorie Barton, and Brian Palermo (2013) describes some of these truths as "patterns" and "connection points" for developing "story sense." Carmine Gallo (2016) refers to some of them as "storyteller's secrets." This chapter provides 12 fundamental truths that are extremely helpful for those who are starting out on their journey as storytellers.

Truth 1. Everyone is a natural storyteller. And with a little practice, everyone can be not just a good but a great storyteller!

You might be thinking, "But that just isn't me. I could never be a great storyteller." It may require a bit of a change in your comfort zone, but it is much easier to accomplish than you think. Chapter 4 will help you choose stories to tell. Start simply by telling a single story. Observe the impact on your audience, and you will be anxious to tell a second story and then a third. If you have read this far into the book, then you are on board with these ideas—or at least with keeping a foot in the door. So it is time to take the plunge: Your journey as a great storyteller begins right now!

Truth 2. A story is infinitely more compelling than data.

"What? We are educated teachers, staff, and administrators! We love data, and we love making data-driven decisions!" That may be true, but the harsh reality is that your audience will glaze over within minutes if you are regurgitating data. Those same audience members will be on the edge of their seats if you are telling a story.

The title of a book by Lori Silverman sums it up perfectly: *Wake Me Up When the Data Is Over: How Organizations Use Storytelling to Drive Results* (Silverman, 2006). In a similar vein, Randy Olson wrote another book targeting scientists who love data: *Don't Be Such a Scientist: Talking Substance in an Age of Style* (Olson, 2009).

Truth 3. There is nothing wrong with being human and showing some emotion when telling a story.

Many educators communicate on a level that only involves the head and the brain and then expect students to stay engaged. But if you want your message to be compelling, be impactful, and truly resonate with the audience, come down out of your head and speak with your heart and your gut. Appeal to the emotions of your audience.

Both teachers and students are human and think with hearts and guts outside of school. So why should teachers silence their hearts, guts, and emotions just because they have entered an educational setting? Your students bring their hearts and guts to school, so why not tell stories that play on the emotions at a more human and personal level?

For example, in biology and beginning allied health, it is important for students to get comfortable with metric units and to understand that the difference between a gram and a milligram is a thousandfold. Would it make a big difference if a patient who should be getting 50 milligrams of a drug accidentally received 50 grams instead?

To make the point about the importance of understanding metric units, you could tell the story of how Dennis Quaid, the famous actor, had infant twins who ended up in the hospital with staph infections in 2007. To prevent blood clots, the twins were given heparin, a common blood thinner. Unfortunately, the hospital staff made a serious error and administered not 10 units but 10,000 units of heparin to each infant.

Soon the twins were bleeding out of every puncture wound where they had received injections, and they began showing bruises all over their tiny bodies. As soon as the error was discovered, emergency treatment was initiated to reverse the effects, but the infants remained in critical condition for the next two days. The twins were finally well enough to come home after 12 days in the hospital. Dennis Quaid and his wife first told this story on the TV news show *60 Minutes* (CBS News, 2008), and Dennis continues to be an outspoken patient-safety advocate.

Why does telling this story make a difference? It has all the emotional components necessary to make it engaging and compelling, including babies on the brink of death, a famous celebrity who has no control over the situation, and a serious case of human error. Students who hear the story never forget it, and therefore never forget the original message about the importance of learning the metric system.

Truth 4. Most people have a short attention span.

Many teachers lament the fact that their students can't stay on task for very long. But it isn't just little kids or middle school kids or high school students or even college students who have short attention spans: It is almost everyone, regardless of age. (You can probably remember a moment in the last month when you were supposed to be paying attention but got bored and distracted and let your mind wander.)

Telling stories instead of regurgitating data is one of the best ways to keep your audience engaged. But even with a story, some people zone out. As a result, it is critical to stay on track with your story so that you don't lose your audience.

One way to explain "good" storytelling is to look at an example of "bad" storytelling. If you have spent much time around young children, you know that they love to tell stories. In their world, life is all about stories! But they have not yet mastered the art of storytelling. So their stories drone on and on; they lose the point of the story, get off track, and wander into unrelated stories.

If you tell stories to your students in the same way, you will lose your audience, just as you may glaze over when listening to a child's story. (And remember, if children can grow up to become good storytellers as adults, then you can certainly become a great storyteller yourself!)

Therefore, it is important to keep your stories concise, on track, and leading to a point or a resolution. That's why TED, one of the most popular forums for storytellers today, sets a limit of 18 minutes for a presentation. Do you think that 18 minutes is too short to convey a message? TED curator Chris Anderson imposed the time limit, saying it is "long enough to be serious and short enough to hold people's attention. By forcing speakers who are used to going on for 45 minutes to bring it down to 18, you get them to think about what they really want to say" (Fisher, 2014).

In fact, you have probably heard the quote (attributed to many different people over the years) "If you want me to talk for a couple of hours, I'm ready right now. If you only want me to talk for a few minutes, I'll need a couple of weeks to prepare." That's why it is important to practice telling your stories.

Speaking of practicing how to tell stories, look at some of the greatest storytellers of all time: stand-up comedians, those who often have only a short time on stage to deliver their act. They need to be focused, stay on track, and make sure their jokes are engaging and compelling. Therefore, they practice for hours and hours for sometimes just five minutes on stage.

Do you think five minutes is a short period of time? Think about a TV commercial that can tell a story in just one minute, or even thirty seconds. And here is the ultimate in telling a story quickly: Check out the top-viewed five-second films at 5secondfilms.com. (Warning: Some of these are rather crude. But they provide some great examples of telling a story in less time than it takes to read this sentence.)

Truth 5. A story begins when something happens.

All stories have a beginning, a middle, and an end. However, given truth 4 above (which states that audiences often have short attention spans), it is important to start your story in a way that quickly grabs the attention of the audience. Olson, Barton, and Palermo (2013) give a great example of the ways that short attention spans have changed how Hollywood starts a story. They look at three big Hollywood disaster movies: *Airport* (1975), *Outbreak* (1995), and *Contagion* (2011).

The movie *Airport* is 136 minutes long, with 84 minutes of backstory before anything happens. (Today, that sounds like a snoozefest!) *Outbreak* is just a little shorter—127 minutes—but the action starts after only 23 minutes. *Contagion*, being typical of many action-adventure films today, starts with intense action in the very first scene, and the entire movie is only 106 minutes long. (No wonder our students today are rarely interested in watching "old" movies from the 20th century!)

What is the takeaway for storytellers? Keep the backstory and setup to a minimum. Jump right into something that grabs the audience so that you hook the audience like you would a fish. Fill in the important backstory details along the way, while you reel people in. Plan the telling of your story ahead of time—start with a bang, stay on track, get to the point—and you will have your audience in the palm of your hand.

Truth 6. *One* is the most powerful number.

This may sound like a sad commentary on human psychology, but it is a cold hard fact. The story of one person is more impactful than the story of two people and much more impactful than the story of 100 people or 1,000 people, or 1,000,000 people. For example, an estimated 500,000 to 1,000,000 people were slaughtered in Rwanda in 1994 in what the history books call the Rwandan genocide. Approximately 6,000,000 Jews were killed during World War II.

An estimated 50,000,000 to 100,000,000 people died of the flu during the pandemic of 1918–1920. One hundred million people! Can you imagine what that was like? Honestly, most people can't get their head around these numbers, and the numbers rarely have the effect on an audience that you might expect. However, if you can tell a story of just one person's experiences in these events, you will make a much greater impact.

Few people in this country paid attention to news reports about the number of deaths in Rwanda in 1994, but the movie *Hotel Rwanda* was viewed by millions and was nominated for multiple Academy Awards. From World War II, one of the most impactful and compelling books about the plight of Jews was *The Diary of a Young Girl*, by Anne Frank, a gripping personal story by a child—a story that readers of all ages could relate to.

As for the 1918 flu pandemic, textbooks give the numbers of victims who were infected and numbers who died, but these numbers have little meaning to most readers. Far more effective are the first-person accounts from survivors, describing what it was like to helplessly watch their children, siblings, parents, friends, and much of their community die. Therefore, the "Pandemic Influenza Storybook" on the CDC website (CDC, 2014), which contains personal stories written by survivors, is far more compelling than any biology, history, or medical textbook account of the pandemic.

Nicholas Kristof (2009) explains it clearly and simply: "One death is a tragedy. A million deaths is a statistic." (His article is a must-read for storytellers.)

Truth 7. The power of the story rests in the details.

Although truth 4 admonishes storytellers to keep stories short, you want to be sure to keep the important details in your stories. The trick is to know what is important. For example, details like the color of the shirt you were wearing in the story is not important (unless the color of the shirt was the focus of the story, because it attracted bees or butterflies and led to something painful or funny).

But the details about what you did in a crucial moment, or the first thoughts that went through your head—these are precisely the details that engage the audience. You will know if your story needs more details if your audience asks questions about the details. If that happens, remember what they asked and include those details the next time you tell the story.

Here's an idea to keep in the back of your mind while you plan and practice your story. We've all heard the late-night talk-show hosts say to the audience, "It was bad!" The audience, in unison, asks, "How bad was it?" The host answers, "It was so bad, that . . ." You get the drift! The audience wants those details.

Here's something that happened to a biology teacher—a story that will resonate with all teachers who have ever felt like they stuck their foot in their mouth! First, the story without details: The teacher was explaining the inheritance of a genetic disease to a class, but he didn't think to ask the students first if they knew anyone who had the disease. That story might be a bit intriguing, but it is not an engaging story because there are no details.

Now here is the story with details this time: The teacher was describing the inheritance of Huntington's disease to his biology class and told the story of Nancy Wexler (discussed earlier in this book). He explained that a parent with Huntington's has a 50% chance of passing it along to his or her children and emphasized just how hard it is on families to care for someone with Huntington's.

After about four seconds of silence (a pause on the teacher's part to let the information sink in), a male student in the class suddenly blurted out, "My mom was just diagnosed with Huntington's a couple months ago." At this instant, the entire class was even more engaged than they had been just seconds before!

Did the story with details catch your attention? Are you wondering what everyone in the room was thinking? Are you wondering about the expressions on the other students' faces as it sinks in that this 20-year-old student has just told the entire class that he has suddenly figured out that he has a 50% chance of dying a horrible death from Huntington's? Are you wondering about the expression on the face of this young man who is suddenly the focal point of all the emotion and sympathy of the entire class? Those very details are the ones that matter in this story!

And while you are wondering about these details, here is the rest of the story: The teacher paused, looked directly at the student, and said, "I am so sorry! So sorry for your family, so sorry for the situation you are in, and so sorry that I didn't stop to ask ahead of time if anyone knew anyone with Huntington's. That was really insensitive of me."

Then the teacher paused, turned to the class, and said, "This is why stories about genetic diseases—and all diseases—are so important. They're not just a list of symptoms or discussions about causes and treatments. They're stories of how these diseases affect our friends, our families, and ourselves."

In addition to this being an example of why details are important, is there a moral to the story? Perhaps the moral is that even when you get to the point that you feel comfortable in telling stories that you've told before, think carefully about how your story can impact individuals in the audience. Would it be better not to tell stories? Absolutely not! The stories engage the students and give relevance to the concepts. Stories give people the power to change the world. But just keep in mind how impactful your story can be. It will be a long time before the 29 people who were in that biology classroom forget what they were feeling at that moment.

Truth 8. Superlatives are the best!

Superlatives describe the extremes: the biggest or the smallest, the most or the least, or the best or the worst. As Olson, Barton, and Palermo (2013) explain it, superlatives make the difference between "one of" the best things about storytelling, and "the" best thing about storytelling. Remember back in truth 7, the audience wanted to know, "How bad was it?" The audience will be more engaged if your story is about the worst ever and not just one of the worst.

Generally, scientists are some of the worst about avoiding superlatives. Oops, that should be restated: Scientists are always the worst when it comes to avoiding superlatives! Why? Perhaps it is because they are trained to keep an open mind and show the audience that they have an open mind. How could something definitely be the biggest beyond a doubt if there is a chance that tomorrow we will find an even bigger version of that something?

And speaking of generalities, saying "generally," "usually," "one of the," or "typically," among others, takes the fun and the appeal out of the story. As a result, scientists don't generate much interest when they say, "This was one of the more interesting discoveries I've made." But instead, if they said, "This is the most amazing discovery I've ever made—perhaps the most amazing discovery in the sciences in the last 50 years!" then the audience would perk up and listen.

Truth 9. If you care, then the audience will care.

Even better: If you care about the story and you have refined the story to make a point and you stay on track when telling the story, then the audience will care. Or put even more thoroughly: If you care about the story, and you keep in mind all the truths discussed in chapter 3, then the audience will definitely care.

Olson, Barton, and Palermo (2013) give an excellent example of a story that most of us expect audiences to care about yet find that they sometimes don't seem to care as much as we think they should. And that is the story of the six million Jews killed during World War II. Shortly after the war, when the world finally had the opportunity to see inside the concentration camps, people flocked to the new concentration camp museums.

Few people visiting the museums were interested in the stories of individual people who had either died in or survived the concentration camps. Why? It was because so many people in Europe knew someone firsthand who had a personal story about the experience. Individual stories just did not draw visitors. Therefore, the emphasis in the museums was about the numbers who were held in the camps, the numbers who were tortured, and the numbers who died.

But over time, as the familiarity of the war began to fade and as new generations came along, people began losing interest in the numbers. As you might expect from truth 6, the fate of six million people was quickly becoming just a statistic. Over the years, as the crowds at the museums began to diminish, the curators of the museums realized they needed to change the narrative. They needed to start retelling the stories of individuals. They needed to share the personal stories of families torn apart, of living in unbelievable and unspeakable horror, and of how and why people did what they did and made the decisions they made.

Today, the museums focus on the stories of individuals, because these are what engage the audience (truths 2 and 6). The stories of the victims play on the emotions of the audience (truth 3). The stories start with the suffering (truth 5) and then add the details that the audience wants to hear (truth 7). Only when the next generation hears the stories of individuals can the audience understand why this was the worst genocide in modern history (truth 8). When the stories are told in this way, then, yes, the audience cares.

Truth 10. It is important to build trust with your audience so that they will believe the story.

The reverse is also true: Telling your audience stories is a great way to make a connection and build trust toward you in the hearts of the audience. Remember from truth 3 that your audience members are thinking with their heart and their gut more than they are thinking with their head. And trust is a gut feeling, not a function of the brain.

Those who have ever taught in a classroom, coached a team, or tried to win the respect of the parents of their charges know that trust is critical and can take time to develop. Therefore, always tell true stories. Always tell stories from the heart. Be willing to tell stories that may show some of your own vulnerability. This will help you build trust with the audience. And once you have that trust, the audience will believe you.

Truth 11. You don't want to sound like a robot.

This truth is basically about acting skills. But even if you don't feel comfortable with being an actor and think you can't learn these skills, there are plenty of things you can do to avoid sounding like a robot. Don't think about how you talk to people at work; instead, think about how you talk to your closest friends at a party. You smile, you laugh, and you use inflections in your voice. You talk with your hands, using lots of gestures. You are animated, and your personality shows through.

Now, just accept that the way you talk to your friends is the real you. Then simply remember to be the real you when you are telling stories at work, talking to students, staff, administrators, parents, and the community. Remember, you are not competing for an Oscar but are just making your stories engaging. Have fun while you tell the stories, and your audience will listen. That's enough to make you a great storyteller.

Truth 12. Everyone can be a great storyteller!

Wait—wasn't that truth 1? Yes! But this truth is twice as important as all the others, especially if it gets you to believe in yourself and to believe that you can change your life, change the lives of your students, and change the direction of your school. It will take some hard work, but it is fun work—and meaningful work. You will be able to see the results simply by watching the expressions of those who listen to your stories. You will know right away that you are accomplishing something worthwhile.

Not only that, you will find that your enjoyment and enthusiasm about stories will also improve your personal life, away from school. Just as you hope that your students become more metacognitive and think about their learning, you will find that you become more metacognitive about everything from the movies you watch to the books you read to the commercials you see on TV. It can even improve your conversations with friends and family. And it is all because your brain is wired for story and because you are now on a journey to becoming a great storyteller.

KEY POINTS FROM CHAPTER 3

There are 12 fundamental truths about great stories and storytelling that all storytellers should keep in mind when they are crafting a compelling and impactful story that resonates with the audience:

1. Everyone is a natural storyteller, and with a little practice, everyone can be a great storyteller.
2. A story is infinitely more compelling than data.

3. Your story will be more impactful if it appeals to the emotions of the audience.
4. Most people have short attention spans, so keep your stories short.
5. A story begins when something happens.
6. The story of one person is more impactful than the story of two, 100, or 1,000,000 people.
7. The power of the story rests in the details.
8. Superlatives are the best!
9. If you care, then your audience will care.
10. Build trust with your audience and they will believe your story.
11. Don't sound like a robot when you tell your story. Try using some basic acting skills.
12. Everyone can be a great storyteller. This is the same as truth 1, repeated because it is the most important truth.

Chapter Four

Choosing Stories to Tell

How do you choose the stories to tell? Since tying a story to a concept is such a powerful tool for learning, you will want to choose stories that are relevant applications and examples of the concepts you want your audience to learn. You may not have realized it yet, but you already have a thorough understanding of this process because you have used, followed, or written learning objectives for teaching.

When you are following a set of learning objectives, you focus only on the concepts that relate to those learning objectives. Anything that doesn't tie into those learning objectives gets left out. Follow the same rule for choosing stories. Choose stories that are examples and applications of the concepts you want to teach. If a story isn't a clear example or application of the concept, then it isn't the right story to tell.

Think for a moment about your life outside of an educational setting. You already have a repertoire of stories that you tell to friends, family, and even strangers. Perhaps you have a story about how your two-year-old daughter colored nearly her entire body with a permanent blue marker; or the time that your grandmother was cooking chokecherries in a pressure cooker to make jelly, released the pressure valve too early, and ended up with the white walls and ceiling of her kitchen covered in sticky purple goo; or the time your friend had too much to drink and threw up all over the inside of your car.

When do you tell these stories? You tell them when you are having a conversation with others—when you are literally swapping stories. Your conversation will most likely have a theme. When it is your turn to tell a story, you will immediately choose one from your repertoire that fits the current theme. You won't just blurt out a completely unrelated story! You may even have a story that ties into more than one theme, so you might tell the same story in multiple conversations and settings but with the story phrased a little differently to fit that theme.

For example, you might tell the story about your daughter and the permanent marker during a conversation about how hard it is to getting marks and stains off skin and clothes, about how your kids have embarrassed you in front of your parents or the pediatrician, or simply about the funny things kids do.

You might tell the story about Grandma and the pressure cooker when the conversation is about canning food, about kitchen accidents, or about the funny things grandparents do.

You might tell the story about your friend who had too much to drink when the theme is what the worst messes to clean up are, the consequences of drinking too much alcohol, or even the lengths we go to in the name of friendship. In fact, you might even bring the story up in the company of that same friend, just as a reminder that he or she "owes you one."

Now put yourself back into an educational setting. You have an almost infinite number of stories to tell. They could be historical stories, stories based on current events, or even personal stories, things that have happened to you. Think about your learning objectives and about what concepts really call for good stories that will make the concepts "stick." Whatever story you pick to tie to a concept, just follow the 12 truths outlined in chapter 3, and your story will be magic.

HISTORICAL STORIES

Stories from history are a great place to start when you are new to storytelling. Textbooks in almost every subject mention historical events at some point. Even if your audience members think they know the story, you can still take that story, build on it, flesh it out, and turn the narrative into a compelling story that resonates. Choose a story with some irony or a story that has a main character who does something heroic or has to make a very difficult decision. Choose a story that has implications today or has had an important influence on something that interests your audience.

For example, in a psychology class, the theories of Carl Jung are important concepts, but to many students, Jung is just another name to memorize. You can make the life of Jung resonate with students by telling the story of how he helped the Allies during WWII. Jung was "Agent 488" and worked with the Office of Strategic Services (a precursor of the CIA) to provide valuable intelligence on the psychological condition of Adolf Hitler (Dickey, 2016).

There is also more to learning about Jung than just the historical stories. The music lovers in your audience will be interested to hear that Jungian ideals were an important source of inspiration for many of the songs by musician David Bowie (Stark, 2015). Want to pique the interest of the video gamers in your classroom? Both the Persona series and the Nights into Dreams series of video games are based on Jung's theories (James, 2015; Valentine, 2010). You can flesh out these stories in order to engage students who may otherwise think of Jung as simply an "old dead guy in the textbook."

In a biology class, when covering the topic of fermentation, you can talk about Johnny Appleseed. Johnny Appleseed was an actual figure from American history. His real name was John Chapman; he was born in Massachusetts in 1774. In the early 1800s, he was well known for giving away apple seeds and seedlings. But the interest in his apple seeds and apple trees was not for apples to eat.

In fact, apples at that time were generally small and bitter. Most of the varieties we eat today are the result of crossbreeding and artificial selection in the last 100 years. Rather, the interest in apples in Johnny Appleseed's day was less about food and more about drink—hard cider, to be exact. At that time, drinking-water sources were often not safe, and water-borne illnesses were common. It was much safer to drink alcohol, even for children, and apples were an excellent source of the sugar needed for alcoholic fermentation.

In addition to tying the story of Johnny Appleseed to fermentation, the story can be a great introduction to a variety of other topics, such as community health problems or the role of artificial selection in our food crops. In fact, a story that can be tied to multiple concepts creates a great opportunity for learning across the discipline. You can revisit the story of Johnny Appleseed when you cover natural and artificial selection, community health, and microbes in drinking water. Every time you relate the story to a different aspect of biology, you are revisiting and reinforcing important concepts.

In addition, a story that can be tied to multiple concepts is a great tool for interdisciplinary learning—that is, across a variety of subject areas. Even if you teach only biology or only history, a discussion of Johnny Appleseed's story makes a great link between the two subjects. These linkages increase student understanding, help students practice their critical-thinking skills, and can lay the foundation for interdisciplinary learning communities.

Speaking of history, history is probably the subject area that most naturally lends itself to storytelling. Many teachers (especially AP teachers in high school) lament that history curricula are too focused on names, dates, and places in order to pass a test. Having to cover so many facts in class has reduced the time available for storytelling.

But storytelling is perfect for the teaching and learning of history. All of us have had many history teachers over the years, generally starting in middle school or even elementary school. When you think back on all those teachers and their teaching methods, the ones you remember more fondly are the storytellers. They made history come alive, and you likely remember many of those stories to this day.

Let's use the example again of the Johnny Appleseed story. A history class is an obvious place to tell this story. And it is a great story to use to help students understand the culture and economics of that time period. In fact, just like the example of potentially using this story in biology for both intradisciplinary and interdisciplinary learning, this story can accomplish the same goals in a history class.

STORIES FROM CURRENT EVENTS

Another source of ideas for stories is the reporting of current events, including television, magazines, social media, and other news sources. The main goal of all of these platforms is to share stories, and these are often the stories that your audience is seeing and hearing every day. So why not incorporate these stories into your teaching? Just keep your eyes and ears open for stories that are examples or applications of the concepts you already teach. Learn the details of the stories, follow the 12 truths from chapter 3, and shape the narratives into stories that will resonate with your students.

An example of a story from the news from a few years ago is the story, described in chapter 3, of Dennis Quaid's twins receiving too much heparin in the hospital. The story was presented as an example of a tie-in to learning about the metric system as a biology/allied health concept. But it can also be tied into learning about blood-clotting in a biology class or learning about common mistakes in an allied health class or even learning about a precedent in a case law class.

RESEARCHING THE DETAILS OF A STORY

Where do you find the details of a story that you have seen or heard in the news? It is common for teachers to fear that the research required for accurate storytelling will take a great deal of time—time that teachers don't have. But it takes less time than you think to gather the information you need. Start with what you heard, read, or saw in the first news report. A quick Google search should yield some corroborating reports from reliable sources.

How much detail do you need? Again, follow the truths from chapter 3. You want enough details to keep the story engaging (truth 7), but you want to keep the story short enough to keep your audience engaged (truth 4). Many stories can be adequately researched and developed in only 20 to 30 minutes. Once you have researched and developed the story, it will be in your story repertoire for as long as you teach.

If you are researching a historical story, or even a story surrounding a current event, another source for researching the details is . . . brace yourself . . . Wikipedia. Yes, Wikipedia. Although most teachers tell their students that Wikipedia is not a reliable source for research, especially when a research project calls for citing primary sources, the reality is that Wikipedia is generally accurate enough to provide a quick place to start your research for a story.

When using Wikipedia, just look critically at the information, follow the references (most of which will contain links to other online sources), and corroborate the details as needed. Wikipedia helps make it easy to find a story and prepare your presentation for teaching a concept the next day.

TELLING PERSONAL STORIES

Once you are comfortable telling stories, you will be ready to tell your own stories. You do not need to start off with overly personal stories that might be a bit embarrassing. Instead, start with the stories about yourself that are simple and straightforward. For example, when teaching the chemistry and biology of carbohydrates, a biology teacher could tell a personal story about hiking, to illustrate the storage and use of glycogen.

When carbohydrates are consumed, the extra sugar molecules in the bloodstream are converted into glycogen, a polysaccharide stored in the muscles and liver. When blood sugar drops too low (during physical activity or before the next meal), glycogen can be converted back into glucose, and put into the bloodstream. (That's why you can feel very hungry, with your stomach growling, but 15 minutes later feel that the intense hunger is gone.) Consuming a big bowl of pasta the evening before running a marathon, called "carbo-loading," is a common way of boosting glycogen stores.

But this concept will stick with students a little better if there is a story that serves as an example. This particular biology teacher was hiking across the Grand Canyon—South Rim to North Rim (23 miles total, hiking a mile down in elevation and more than a mile back up to the other side)—in a single day. The teacher brought food, including jerky, cheese, half a loaf of bread, and a bag of candy.

Halfway up the trail to the North Rim, the teacher was feeling very tired and out of energy. All of the "real" food had already been consumed, and all that was left was candy. Within five minutes of eating a handful of candy (made entirely of simple sugars), the teacher felt a burst of energy, and easily hiked another mile. But the sugar was metabolized quickly, and 30 minutes later the teacher was tired and weak again. Another handful of candy supplied the energy to go another mile, and this continued until the teacher reached the North Rim.

In hindsight, the teacher realized that his glycogen stores were depleted halfway to the North Rim and that the only available blood sugar was coming from the quick processing of simple sugars in the candy. The teacher told this story every semester when covering carbohydrates, and many of his students told him at the end of each semester that they retained the story.

Why does this story work? It is a straightforward story that is a solid example of the concept—a direct application of the chemistry and biology of carbohydrates, including glycogen. It is a quick story to tell, but it has enough detail to be engaging. This is a story that could happen to anyone. In fact, many students can relate the story to a similar experience they have had in their own lives. Another benefit to the story, according to this biology teacher, is that students are always a bit impressed with the fact that he had indeed hiked the Grand Canyon rim to rim in a single day.

When you are feeling completely comfortable with storytelling, you will be ready to tell the more personal stories from your own life. Here is another example from the same biology teacher described above. He wanted to come up with an activity that promoted critical thinking while students learned something about human physiology. So he created a "case study" based on his daughter's health issues. Instead of telling students from the beginning that this story was about his own daughter, he told them he had found the case study online and read the details to the students as if it were a clinical case.

While this might initially sound like a very unengaging approach, the teacher told the story one step a time, a story about a high-school girl who had symptoms that were difficult to diagnose. Periodically, he stopped the story to ask students to give suggestions on possible diagnoses or to ask their opinion on what to do next. The story gradually unfolded like an episode of *House* (or *House M.D.*), the long-running TV series of a Sherlock Holmes-style doctor who took on difficult cases that other doctors could not solve.

By the end of the story, it was revealed that the girl was eventually diagnosed with Hashimoto's hypothyroiditis and celiac disease and that she had inherited a predisposition for Hashimoto's and a gluten allergy from her father and her paternal grandmother. Thyroid-replacement medication and a switch to a gluten-free diet got her back on track and able to go out of state to college.

But the final twist in the story happens when the teacher said, "And now my daughter is doing very well in college after these diagnoses." Up until that moment, the story was simply about a girl with an interesting medical problem to solve. The fact that the girl in the story was actually the teacher's daughter, and that the teacher himself has a thyroid problem and a gluten allergy, came as a bit of a shock to the students.

The story instantly became even more compelling and engaging, and the students eagerly jumped into the next step of the assignment, which included researching and then reporting on various aspects of Hashimoto's, gluten allergies, and learning to live with these conditions.

Why does this story work? The story of a high-school-aged girl struggling along with her parents to find the source of her health problems hits an emotional chord with the audience. The story unfolds like a book or a movie or an episode of a TV show. The story also shows a more personal side of the teacher and helps to create a stronger bond between the students and the teacher. In fact, students come up to the teacher every semester after completing the case study and want to discuss their own, similar experiences.

Story is always a component of case study, which accomplishes several goals in teaching and learning. The use of the case study, a powerful way to use stories, as illustrated above, will be explored further in chapters 5 and 6.

KEY POINTS FROM CHAPTER 4

- You already have a repertoire of stories that you draw on when swapping personal stories with family and friends. It is time to start gathering stories to tell in your role as an educator.
- Stories can come from historical or current events, or you can tell personal stories.
- Research your stories as needed and practice them ahead of time, and you will always be ready with the right story for every occasion.

Chapter Five

How to Tell Stories in Any Educational Setting

Stories are powerful tools for learning in all teaching modalities, including traditional lecture, online, hybrids, flipped design, and nontraditional settings. How do you tell stories in every one of these different settings? It is easier than you might think.

THE TRADITIONAL LECTURE CLASSROOM

When most people think of a classroom, they might think of the typical K–12 classroom full of kids sitting in rows, with a teacher at the front of the room. Or they may envision a college classroom with anywhere from a couple dozen to several hundred students, with a professor acting as a "sage on the stage." There is nothing wrong with these approaches to teaching and learning. All of us have taken classes in these types of settings. They have been the most common school settings for a very long time and will continue to be an important part of our educational system.

However, the traditional lecture classroom becomes ineffective for learning when things get boring. Again, all of us have experienced boring lectures in large classrooms throughout our educational career. Think back over your experiences as a student in a classroom; chances are that the enjoyable times—when you learned something—were the times you were listening to stories. On the other hand, the times you went to sleep in a classroom were probably the times when the teacher droned on and on with facts and data.

Part of the problem in a traditional classroom is that the students are sitting comfortably—sometimes too comfortably—and they have short attention spans. The headline from a 2015 *Time* article said this: "You Now Have a Shorter Attention Span Than a Goldfish."

The article goes on to say that the average attention span of a goldfish is nine seconds, but a study by Microsoft shows that the average human attention span has decreased from 12 seconds in the year 2000 to just eight seconds today (McSpadden, 2015). Only eight seconds? Now think about how long some of your teachers droned on and on in a traditional lecture classroom!

It is for this reason that storytelling is the single most effective way to make lecture more engaging for students. What is more, storytelling is also the easiest way to make lecture more effective and more engaging for students. Follow the suggestions in chapter 4 for choosing stories and the truths in chapter 3 for effective storytelling, and you can start making your lectures more engaging starting tomorrow.

Are you concerned that making time for stories will take away from precious time to cover content? Just envision yourself lecturing to a classroom full of goldfish with their very short attention spans. If your audience is not engaged, then it really doesn't matter how much content you are presenting or how important it may be.

Storytelling is also the most effective way to make lecture more fun and fulfilling for teachers. Your audience will know if you are having fun and if you are enjoying your role as a teacher. If you are more engaged while telling stories, then your students will be more engaged as well.

Although schools, teachers, and students have many reasons for moving away from traditional lecture and choosing other modalities (like hybrid and online classes), lectures that make good use of storytelling will always be one of the most powerful venues for learning. Indeed, lecturing with storytelling can be extremely effective, while lecturing without storytelling can be a waste of time for all involved. If the traditional lecture classroom is your educational environment, but you are new to storytelling, start integrating some stories right away, and you will quickly notice the benefits.

Is the oral telling of a story the only method for storytelling in a traditional lecture classroom? Of course not. You can use video and other multimedia sources, which will be discussed next.

ONLINE INSTRUCTION

Let's jump to the other extreme: the often impersonal learning environment of online instruction. If you have concerns about student engagement in a traditional lecture classroom, just imagine how unengaged students can be in an online environment, sitting at home alone on their computers, with a world full of distractions just a mouse click away.

It is surprisingly easy to integrate stories into online instruction. In fact, you can divide your approach to storytelling into two categories: stories that you yourself tell and stories you find that have been told by others. For example, you can incorporate a video clip into your course materials, either a recording of you telling a story or a video of someone else telling a story.

Video is one of the easiest ways to add stories to your online course, and you don't have to be an expert on making videos. YouTube and other sites already contain millions of short video clips that you can integrate into your course materials. Look for clips that have some impactful narration, show some emotion, and grip the audience.

The best length for a video clip depends on the subject and content, but a clip of five to 10 minutes is often sufficient to engage students, keep their attention, and tell a story. If the video clip needs a set-up, you can supply the background text for students to read before they watch the clip.

How much set-up does a video clip need? The best answer is: enough setup to tie the story to the concept. Again, the story is only meaningful if you tie it to a concept in your course. You provide the materials to teach the concept, you provide the explanation that ties the concept to the story, and then either you or someone else tells the story with a video clip.

The use of video clips in online instruction, or for that matter, in any modality of instruction, has many benefits. Many of your audience members are probably part of the "YouTube Generation" and watch short videos all day long, including videos on platforms such as Facebook and Reddit. Therefore, video is already what much of your audience is using for learning every day.

Video clips also help break up your curricular materials into smaller chunks of information, providing a change of pace from reading assignments. And finally, video as a medium can include all the components that help make a story more compelling, including images, narration, and music.

But video is not the only storytelling tool you can use in online instruction. Podcasts (and other audio formats) can also relay a relevant and compelling story, and many of your students already make audio a part of everyday life. Think about how often students walk into your school or even your classroom with earbuds or headphones. They are already comfortable dealing with downloading and playing audio files. In fact, when your students walk in with earbuds, you may assume they are listening to music, but they could indeed be listening to podcasts.

Podcasts are becoming more popular with many adult learners today. In a 2017 article, *Forbes* cited data indicating that at least 112,000,000 Americans have listened to podcasts, up 11% from the year before, with 67,000,000 Americans listening to podcasts each month (DeMers, 2017).

Why are podcasts becoming more popular? There have always been people who enjoy listening to spoken audio, and audiobooks have been around for years as cassette tapes and CDs. Many people listen to them at home or while in the car. The availability of shorter content in a podcast (shorter than a multi-CD audiobook) attracts additional listeners. Combine that with the ease of downloading a podcast to a smartphone, with no need for a CD or cassette player, and podcasts become even more appealing.

Finally, in the current climate of entertainment on demand (a big change from the days that older generations remember, when you had to turn on the television or radio at the right time in order to catch your favorite show), a podcast lets you listen on your own schedule. The popularity of many of the NPR radio shows continues to increase as more people choose podcasts as a flexible way of listening.

As a result, podcasts can be an extremely effective way to engage students in an online class. You can find free stories in podcast form on NPR, in iTunes, and from many other sources, and give the link(s) to your students. You may also want to consider recording your own podcasts for your class. Recording video is easy enough these days, with little needed other than a smartphone and/or a laptop, but recording an audio podcast is even easier. (And you don't even need to change out of your pajamas—your students will never know!)

In addition to video and podcasts, you can include stories in written form. With the number of people who blog constantly rising and the trend for major publishers of print media to duplicate their articles online, there is an almost infinite source of stories out there for your students to read. Many of these stories contain photos and other images as well. This low-tech avenue, providing a link to an online story for your students to read, is the fastest way to include stories in your online curriculum.

HYBRID INSTRUCTION

A hybrid class can be defined in a variety of ways, but it nearly always means that there is some in-class and/or in-person learning combined with an online learning component. This instructional modality can be the best of both worlds when it comes to both teaching and learning. The trick to a successful hybrid class is to put the most basic reading and learning components into online delivery and save the most impactful activities for the classroom meetings. These activities can include class discussions, hands-on labs, and problem-solving activities.

In-class activities in a hybrid class should also include your best teaching moments: those explanations that you provide in a classroom setting that help explain difficult concepts. Most teachers have a repertoire of these well-rehearsed standards that are always the most effective when delivered in real time and face to face with students. These teaching moments should also include your best stories, the ones that always captivate your students, provide the perfect relevant application for a concept, and generate a response ranging from laughter to tears.

In fact, a hybrid class meeting can be the perfect opportunity to deliver an entire multimedia storytelling experience. For example, a college teacher used the topic of wolves as a case study activity in the community ecology module of his environmental biology class. The students came to class with some knowledge of community ecology thanks to the online work they completed before class. Learning the basics of community ecology before class meant that the teacher could skip the detailed lecture on the core material and jump straight into the story.

On the day that the wolf case study took place, students would walk into a dark and quiet classroom and sense that something unusual was about to happen. Even before the class meeting was scheduled to begin, the teacher would start an MP3 audio file of mournful wolf howls, using his phone plugged into the classroom sound system. The howls would continue for about five minutes, with no one saying a word. Then the teacher would read (dramatically!) a story written by Aldo Leopold called "Thinking Like a Mountain." (This short story has been posted online on many ecology-related websites, and is easy to find.)

In this story, Leopold describes in detail the pain he feels after shooting a wolf and watching the "fierce green fire dying in her eyes." The story only takes about five minutes to tell, including long pauses for dramatic effect. When the story was finished, the teacher would let the recording of the howls continue for another five minutes, while students quietly reflected on what they had heard. Then the discussion would begin.

This introduction to the case study was always extremely impactful. In less than 15 minutes, the teacher had used an audio of wolf howls and a dramatic reading of a story to set up the day's activity in an engaging way. Every student was awake, alert, and ready to participate. In fact, this introduction would often lead in different directions, depending on the audience and even the mood of the teacher. Sometimes a brief history lesson would follow, explaining the life and teachings of Aldo Leopold.

Next, the teacher would have students begin doing online research on the impact of wolf extinction and reintroduction at Yellowstone National Park and would follow up with class discussion. Occasionally, the class discussion would even include the students' experiences of hunting, if at least a few of the students were hunters. Regardless of where the activity headed during the class meeting, the teacher always felt it was extremely effective and engaging and that the key to success was starting with the story.

THE "FLIPPED" CLASSROOM

A "flipped" classroom is a popular modality for teaching sciences but can be used in a variety of subject areas. It is very similar to hybrid instruction, with both online learning and in-class components. In a typical flipped design, the lecture material is moved into online delivery (often including video and/or podcasts) for students to learn before coming to class. Like hybrid instruction, this allows more time for activities during class time.

In a science class, the increase in time for activities often means that hands-on wet labs can be done without rushing the students. In any subject area, it also means that what used to be considered individual homework can now be done in a small group setting, with the teacher present in the room to provide help and answer questions. Many teachers who have used this method feel that engagement among students has increased and learning has improved.

If you use a flipped approach in your course, you can see that using class time for storytelling could be extremely effective. In fact, in addition to your storytelling, you can also use the opportunity to have students tell stories. Just as understanding can improve when students do homework in small groups, where they can help each other, so can students benefit from hearing the stories of other students. Again, the beauty of the hybrid and flipped approaches is that the online portion of the learning allows for more time in the classroom.

Let's talk about stories told by students. If you have taught elementary school, particularly grades K–3, you know that opening the door to having students telling stories can be risky at best. Kids love to tell stories at that age; in fact, their entire world is all about stories. There is no faster way to lose control of your classroom than to let kids tell stories. As a result, many teachers are afraid to provide regular opportunities for them to do so.

However, stories told by students can be powerful at any grade level. Part of the job of the teacher can be to help even the youngest students find their voices and become great storytellers. Methods for empowering students to tell their own stories will be covered in chapter 9.

NONTRADITIONAL EDUCATIONAL SETTINGS

Education also happens outside of traditional classrooms and schools. Perhaps you train employees for a company. Maybe you work in a museum, preparing exhibits. Perhaps you are in the role of a coach or mentor or do one-on-one tutoring or run educational workshops for teachers or students. All of these are educational roles, and you are, in fact, a teacher. Storytelling in these nontraditional settings is still the best way to engage your audience and help them learn.

While discussing various teaching and learning modalities in this chapter, the following storytelling tools have been described:

- teacher-told stories in a classroom,
- video stories, either produced by the teacher or using video clips found online,
- audio stories, either produced by the teacher or using podcasts found online,
- text-based stories with images, either produced by the teacher or found online in blogs or on the websites of major media publishers, and
- stories told by students.

Just as these are all options when teaching in traditional or online environments, so can they all be useful tools if you are teaching in nontraditional settings. Here are some examples of nontraditional educational settings where storytelling can help. Perhaps some of these examples will sound familiar.

Have you ever been to a museum and been bored out of your mind? Think of times when you did not feel engaged, such as when you were looking at displays filled with artifacts but had no context for why you should care about the artifacts.

Now think of a trip to a museum that you enjoyed. Chances are that there were stories being told about how the artifacts were used, who made and used them, or how they ended up in the museum. Was it an emotional story of suffering? Was it an exciting story of risk and adventure? For a visitor, stories told in a museum can mean the difference between seeing nothing but a room full of junk and seeing a room full of treasures.

Have you had to sit through a boring training workshop at your place of employment? Many employees cringe at the thought of an employer-led training session. (Why is it that school employees who provide training for teachers often model the worst in teaching practices?) Why is the information being taught important? What are the consequences if you don't follow the suggestions or rules presented? Just as a story makes a concept relevant and applicable in a classroom, so can it add relevance during training and keep the audience engaged.

Have you ever gotten a traffic ticket and had to attend a defensive driving class? You will likely hear long lists of statistics about numbers of accidents, injuries, and deaths. But just like in a traditional educational setting, the audience will lose interest if the only thing that is presented is statistics. If you find yourself teaching in this situation, your audience will zone out upon hearing data on the number of injuries and deaths that result from texting while driving, but one gripping story of a death due to texting will stay with your audience for years.

Have you ever been in the role of an athletics coach? Although many adults today thrive on sports statistics, these stats are often meaningless to young athletes. What kids remember are the stories of athletes who overcome adversity and always give it their best. Why is it important to stretch first, keep your gear clean, or practice every day? Tie a story to what you teach, and your students will always keep your training in mind.

As you can see, there are many ways to integrate stories into your teaching, regardless of the teaching and learning modality or environment. For a small investment in preparation time, you can greatly improve the effectiveness of your teaching and the engagement of your audience. Next, let's look at ideas for weaving stories into your lectures, discussions, and activities.

KEY POINTS FROM CHAPTER 5

- In a traditional classroom, you can be very effective in telling your stories face to face, but be sure to remember the storytelling truths in chapter 3.
- If you teach online, you can record your stories in video format and embed them into your course.
- You can also create audio podcasts of your stories and embed them into your online course.
- For your online course, you can also embed stories told by others as video clips or as digital stories.
- In hybrid or flipped classes, you can make use of both face-to-face storytelling and online stories.
- Basically, all storytelling techniques can be used in nontraditional as well as traditional educational settings.

Chapter Six

Weaving Stories Into Lectures, Discussions, and Activities

As stated in chapter 3, stand-up comedians are some of the world's best storytellers. Watching stand-up comedy is a great way to improve your own storytelling skills by studying the comedian's timing, the audience response, and how the comedian deals with a difficult crowd. But you do not necessarily want to enter your classroom the way a comedian takes the stage! In a comedy club, the audience expects rapid-fire stories that may or may not (!) be appropriate for all ages. And the audience probably just wants to be entertained and is not expecting to learn anything.

The classroom audience's expectations are very different from those of the audience in a comedy club. Your audience expects to learn something but not necessarily be entertained. You can find that middle ground. You can help your audience learn. By your being a storyteller, your students can not only learn but also have fun and be entertained. To accomplish this, simply weave some stories into your lectures, discussions, and class activities.

In chapter 1, there was an example, used in order to put autosomal dominant inheritance in context, of a biology teacher using the story of Nancy Wexler, who found the gene for Huntington's and developed a genetic test. The goal was to describe the concept first and then follow with a story to give the concept relevance. The story was memorable, and it helped students remember the concept.

But there is no rule that says that the concept should be presented first and then followed by the story. You can also start with the story first. In chapter 5, there was an example of an environmental biology teacher who started class with a story about wolves and then jumped into a discussion and a case study about community ecology. In fact, sometimes starting with the story is preferable. The story hooks the students from the beginning and holds their attention throughout the teaching of the concept.

Both approaches—either telling the story first or explaining the concept first—work well. It depends on the concept, the story, the context, the audience, and your personal preference as a teacher and a storyteller. Since the goal is to acquire a repertoire of stories that you use each time you teach the concept, you can always try out both ways and see what works best. Have fun and experiment with different approaches.

CASE STUDIES AND STORIES

Speaking of case studies, and speaking of starting with a story first, the case study method is a great way to use stories in your teaching. Case studies have been used for many years in teaching medicine, law, and business. The use of case studies is brilliantly described and explained in a book by Clyde Freeman Herreid, titled *Start With a Story: The Case Study Method of Teaching College Science* (2007).

Although many examples in his book are about teaching science and teaching at the college level, Herreid's volume is still the best book available on teaching by using cases, and it is extremely valuable for teaching any subject and any grade level. Herreid covers many different approaches to using the case study method, all of which are easily transferable for any topic.

What are cases, and what is the case study method? Herreid explains it succinctly: "Cases are stories with a message. They are not simply narratives for entertainment. They are stories to educate. Humans are storytelling animals. Consequently, the use of cases gives a teacher an immediate advantage; she has the attention of the audience" (Herreid, 2007, chapter 6). Case studies are an extremely effective way to engage students and provide relevance and application for concepts.

Herreid came to view case studies based on stories as a way to improve teaching and learning after his own students and colleagues let him know about their frustrations with their education. A colleague at one of his case study workshops put it in context: "It took me about four years to get over my undergraduate education. All those lectures. All of that memorization. We never really used any of it except to answer test questions. We learned the same thing over and over each semester and never remembered much between one semester and the next, because we never used it" (Herreid, 2007, chapter 2).

She added, "Undergraduate teaching isn't just neutral—it's hurtful" (Herreid, 2007, chapter 2). That is a powerful statement! The goal for teachers should be not only to help students learn but also to spark their interest instead of chasing them away. Unfortunately, students being chased away happens more often than most teachers want to admit. Students come to resent learning blocks of content in certain subjects, or even entire subjects, because the material seems irrelevant and useless.

How many times have you heard a student say, "I hate science classes," or "I can't learn math." Often, this thinking began in a classroom where the teacher was simply ineffective at engaging students and making the content relevant and meaningful. If those students had experienced classes with a few teachers who were better storytellers, then the students might have viewed their education in a very different light. Some of those students might have even changed their career plans and their majors along the way, all because of a great teacher who was a storyteller.

As Herreid describes in his book, case studies based on real stories are widely used in medical schools, law schools, and even business schools. Why? Solving difficult problems and finding answers to questions raised by real-world stories are what these fields are all about. For many doctors, work is all about the cases they see every day, involving patients and their individual stories. Likewise, lawyers deal with cases every day, cases that are based on the stories of their clients.

Even when teaching business topics, there is a need to make topics less ethereal and more practical. There is no better way than to base the teaching and learning on real cases with stories. But it shouldn't stop with just medicine, law, and business. It's important to understand that any subject can be taught with case studies based on real stories.

How long does it take a teacher to become proficient with the case study approach? It is a process, and it takes time. Herreid describes many different types of case study formats, including discussion, debate, public hearing, trial, problem-based learning, scientific research team, team learning—the list seems endless. He also gives detailed explanations on how to find cases and even how to write your own. But here is what every teacher must know: Teaching with case studies always means starting with a story, and you can begin using stories in your teaching today.

This means you can get started immediately in moving toward better methods of teaching. You don't need to jump into a carefully choreographed hours-long, days-long, or weeks-long case study right away. Instead, start with a few stories tied to the concepts you already teach. Get comfortable with finding stories. Get comfortable telling stories. Get some practice integrating your stories into your teaching. As your skills improve in these areas, you will be well on your way to taking the next steps.

Chapter 6

INTERESTING PEOPLE WITH INTERESTING STORIES

Let's take a look again at choosing stories, a discussion started in chapter 4. As stated in chapter 4, you can categorize your stories into historical stories, stories from current events, and personal stories. How do you quickly find a historical story or a story from current events? It is as simple as doing the same type of Internet search that you already do (and probably do several times a day). Start with some very general search terms and see what comes up. Or start in Wikipedia (yes, Wikipedia!) and read a couple of articles on your topic.

When you start your Internet search, look for some aspect of your topic that can be shaped into an interesting story. Did something amazing—or maybe something horrible—happen? Was someone famous involved? Was there any ethical dilemma involved? Did something surprising happen? Look at all the angles, including the lives of the people involved or something that may have been an influence on the people. What was their childhood like? Did they accomplish anything or achieve notoriety for something they did?

People and events in stories become more memorable when you look at their entire lives. Here is an example of someone with an interesting life that makes for a great teaching story. William Marston (1893–1947) was the creator of the DISC Personality System, the inventor of the polygraph machine, and the creator of the Wonder Woman character for DC comics ("William M. Marston," 2018). Interesting facts are available about the two women he lived with, and the four children he fathered with them (Marston, 2017). Tie his story to a concept in psychology, biology, or a related subject, and students will be captivated.

Here is another example. Thomas Midgley Jr. (1889–1944) was the chemist who was responsible for both the addition of lead to gasoline and the use of CFCs as a refrigerant, leading to two of the world's biggest pollution problems of the 20th century. Midgley's story is even more compelling when you look at his own health issues. In an effort to prove that the addition of lead to gasoline was safe, Midgley inhaled the fumes of tetraethyl lead for a full minute at a press conference. He then spent the next several months recovering from lead poisoning (Fourtane, 2018).

But Midgley's story didn't stop there. In 1940, at the age of 51, Midgley contracted polio, which left him disabled. To help himself get out of bed, he invented a system of ropes and pulleys attached to the ceiling. Unfortunately, at age 55, he became entangled in the ropes, and died of asphyxiation (Fourtane, 2018). Midgley's inventions, especially the use of lead in gasoline, hurt many people around the world, but Midgley's final invention took his life. What a story!

What makes stories about people like Marston and Midgley memorable are the ironies and paradoxes in their lives. In fact, it is when you look at the details of the entire life of each person that the stories become even more compelling. These are the details that make their stories engaging and help provide you with links and connections to a variety of different topics and concepts.

Therefore, when you do your Internet search, feel free to wander down whatever path the Internet leads you. Now and then, everyone is guilty of "wasting time" online by continuing to follow links as stories unfold. Or perhaps you have gotten caught up in the YouTube "rabbit hole" by clicking on all of the related and suggested videos. Suddenly you discover that an hour or more has passed! But that is exactly the way that you will find interesting and memorable stories when you search the Internet.

In fact, the more obscure the story, the more engaging your story will be to your audience. You probably don't like it when you're telling a joke and the other person stops you before you are done and gives away the punch line. And no one wants to hear the same joke they have already heard a thousand times. The same is true when you tell a story to your students. Find some lesser-known stories that your students haven't heard before. Even if you tell the same stories every time you teach particular concepts, your stories will still be new to that particular audience.

USING STORIES TO IMPROVE CRITICAL THINKING

All teachers say they want to promote and encourage critical thinking among their students. Using stories in your curriculum is a great method for accomplishing that goal. But first, do you know exactly what "critical thinking" is? Many different definitions have been written by many different authors—just check out some of the definitions at criticalthinking.org.

Let's look at the first definition offered on that site: "Critical thinking is the intellectually disciplined process of actively and skillfully conceptualizing, applying, analyzing, synthesizing, and/or evaluating information gathered from, or generated by, observation, experience, reflection, reasoning, or communication, as a guide to belief and action" ("Defining Critical Thinking," 2017).

That definition is a bit overwhelming! So let's start with a few key words and phrases from that definition in order to create a very simple and basic definition: "Critical thinking [includes] the process of applying, synthesizing, and evaluating information."

Most teachers would be thrilled if they could show that their students regularly apply, synthesize, and evaluate the concepts taught in the class. Again, the use of stories is one of the best ways to accomplish that goal. First of all, a story provides the hook that engages the students. (This is one of the reasons that the "story first" approach is sometimes best.) If the story has an emotional component to which a majority of the students can relate, then the students become invested in the story, its outcome, and therefore the concept you are trying to teach.

If you, as the teacher, show the students how the story is tied to the concept, and if students are invested in the story, then the students will put more thought into the relationship between the story and the concept. You have now set the groundwork for students to use critical thinking to apply the information. You want your students to analyze how well the story provides application and relevance for the concept. At this point, you want to provide students with a chance to reflect on that and perhaps do an activity or an assessment.

Perhaps you pause at this moment and allow students to discuss their thoughts about the story, and the relationship between the story and the concept, either in small groups or as an entire class. Perhaps you provide a short assessment and ask students to explain their thoughts about the relationship between the story and the concept. Perhaps you provide a longer assessment, asking how another similar story does or does not support the concept.

Perhaps the story you provided to the students only skims the surface, and more research will be required in order for students to relate the story to the concept. This is the essence of case studies—they generally push students to gather more information in order to answer a question, solve a problem, or more clearly explain the relationship to the concept. You have now set the groundwork for the next step in the simplified definition of critical thinking: You want the students to synthesize the information they collect from their own research or from working in teams.

The third step in the simplified definition of critical thinking is evaluation. If the students understand how the story applies to the concept, and if they have gathered and synthesized additional information, they are ready for evaluation. Evaluation at this point can take many forms. Do students now see the value of learning the concept in your class? Can they recognize other examples that relate to the concept? Can they cite examples from their own daily lives that relate to the concept? When students reach this point, they are demonstrating critical thinking. They are becoming critical thinkers.

Another thing to consider when using stories to promote critical thinking is the age-old "depth of content" problem. Do you feel that you must cover an enormous amount of material in your class just so that your students will be prepared for the next class or the next grade? That is a common problem for teachers at all grade levels and in nearly every subject. But which is more important for students going into the next class: Should they be walking encyclopedias or critical thinkers?

If you settle on helping to create critical thinkers, then you can take a hard look at modifying your curriculum. Pick out the concepts that are most important. Focus on the critical ones that absolutely must be covered. Find stories that support each of those concepts. In fact, find several different stories that support each of those concepts. Multiple stories help ensure that at least one story for each concept will really resonate with each student. Spread the multiple stories over the entire semester or entire school year to revisit and reinforce those core concepts.

If you cut extraneous content, focus on the core concepts, use stories to support those concepts, and help your students become critical thinkers, you will be the best teacher you can be. Your students will appreciate you as well; they will be more successful in your class and in the classes that follow. You will also be modeling the best in teaching and learning, which will help your students become lifelong learners—and perhaps more of them will go into teaching as a career!

KEY POINTS FROM CHAPTER 6

- Start with a story and then follow with the concept. Or start with the concept and follow with a story. Both methods work fine; just choose the method that feels right.
- The case study method is an excellent approach to showing applications for concepts. Teaching with the case study method always means starting with a story.
- When looking for stories for your course, look for interesting stories about interesting people.
- When students are asked to evaluate the connection between the concepts you teach and the stories you tell, students are demonstrating critical thinking.
- When students relate their own stories to the concepts you are teaching, they are demonstrating critical thinking.
- Take a hard look at everything you teach in your course. There is an immense benefit to cutting extraneous content, focusing on the most important core concepts, and telling stories that support those core concepts.

Chapter Seven

Digital Stories and Video Stories

The use of video stories was described briefly in chapter 5. Video stories are especially useful in online and hybrid learning modalities and are easy to find and incorporate into your curriculum. In fact, it is easier than you might expect to create your own videos. But what are "digital stories"?

Digital storytelling is exactly what it sounds like: stories told in digital format. When you think about all the possibilities for nondigital storytelling, they can include a wide variety of options, including speaking in front of a group, a play in a theater, a photograph on paper, or a painting on canvas. In all of these cases, there is something physical in the form of a person or some physical medium. Digital stories, on the other hand, exist only as electronic files.

The advantage to digital storytelling is the ability to share stories very quickly with a wider audience, using the Internet and social media. While some teachers still prefer physical media and physical delivery, most of today's student audience grew up in a digital environment. Many of your students already view dozens of digital stories every day, yet they probably don't even realize those stories are referred to as "digital."

So back to the question of what exactly digital stories are. Imagine a continuum of storytelling, with a person orally telling a story at one end of the spectrum and a Hollywood blockbuster movie at the other end of the spectrum. The person orally telling a story has very few tools for impactful storytelling: basically, just his or her voice, gestures, facial expressions, and other forms of body language.

At the other end of the spectrum is the big Hollywood movie, which uses every possible tool for storytelling, including actors, additional narration, images, action, music, lighting, and even special effects. Movies can be powerful platforms for telling stories. Just think about how empowered you feel when you walk out of a movie theater after watching a superhero movie.

But these differences between oral storytelling (with just voice and body language) and Hollywood movie storytelling (with all the bells and whistles) certainly do not mean that Hollywood movies are better or that oral storytelling is boring. It depends on how engaging the storyteller is and how engaging the story is. A TED Talk with a storyteller on a stage can change your life, while a bad movie can put you to sleep.

Given those two extremes on the continuum, with oral storytelling at one end and a blockbuster movie at the other end, think of digital storytelling as somewhere in between. The storyteller might create a web page with a story in text format and a few photographs. Or the storyteller might create an audio file to listen to while you view images. Or perhaps the final product might feel like a video, with narration and with slowly moving photographs (think Ken Burns documentary). There could be music in addition to narration. A digital story, then, can be very simple or fairly complex.

To get a feel for what digital storytelling is like, take a look at some digital stories online. When you look at a video, or some text with pictures, on sites like Facebook, that is basically a digital story. But digital storytelling isn't just for social media. Many schools and teachers require students to create digital stories for class assignments. In the past, it was common to have students write a paper about something historical or about some aspect of their own lives. Today, many teachers encourage students to create multimedia digital stories that can be shared with a wider audience.

There are many places where you can view digital stories from school assignments and community projects. One of the pioneers in digital storytelling was the San Francisco Center for Digital Media, started in the early 1990s. In 1998, the center moved to Berkeley and became the Center for Digital Storytelling, a nonprofit community arts organization. In 2015, the organization became StoryCenter (2018): their website can be found at www.storycenter.org—just click on the link for "stories."

One school that emphasizes digital storytelling is the University of Houston. You can find examples of stories created by students by going to www.digitalstorytelling.coe.uh.edu and clicking on the link for "example stories" (Robin, 2018a). The website includes stories in many different categories and subject areas. Some of the stories are historical, while some are extremely personal. The tools used in the stories vary widely. Some include music in addition to narration. Some use video footage, while others use still photos.

But what do all of these digital stories have in common? They are generally short, usually in the four- to six-minute range, although a few are longer, and some are as short as two minutes. There is no correct length; it depends on the story and the media used. If the story is simple, with just a few images, then a shorter length is better. But if the story is compelling and contains more media elements, then a longer length can still keep the viewer engaged.

Another commonality is the narration, almost always the voice of the creator of the digital story and intended to be personal and compelling. However, just as in any other storytelling scenario, from a person on stage to actors in a movie, the delivery of the dialogue can be exciting to hear or it can be stodgily delivered, as if the script is simply being read. When the narration is more exciting, the listener will be more engaged. When the speaker is simply reading a script, the audience will tune out fairly quickly. (This was also covered in truth 11 back in chapter 3.)

Even with these commonalities in digital stories, there is still a great deal of variation. Some stories are based entirely on one photograph or one image. (The use of single images that tell stories will be covered in the next chapter.) Sometimes the photos or images slide across the screen or zoom in or out, or they do both, a technique made famous by filmmaker Ken Burns. In fact, the technique of pan and zoom in his documentaries is now widely known as the Ken Burns effect, and many software programs for creating videos contain "Ken Burns effect" shortcuts.

Another difference among digital stories is the use of a music soundtrack behind the oral narration. Some storytellers use it, and some do not. Music should only be used when it enhances the story and doesn't detract from it. The wrong music or the wrong volume can ruin the storytelling experience. The same holds true for sound effects other than music—they can add to or seriously detract from the story.

There are many sources of suggestions and helpful hints for creating compelling digital stories. One resource is Samantha Morra (2013), who provides six characteristics of great digital stories; according to Morra, digital stories

- are personal,
- begin with the story and script,
- are concise,
- use readily available source materials,
- include universal story elements, and
- involve collaboration at a variety of levels.

Joe Lambert from the Center for Digital Storytelling (now StoryCenter) describes seven elements of digital storytelling (Robin, 2018b), nicely summarized in a digital storytelling video by Paul Iwancio (2010):

1. *Point of view*: What is the point of the story? Who am I telling the story to? Why am I telling the story now? You bring the value of your own personal experience and a unique point of view to the story.

2. *A dramatic question*: Good stories grab and connect the audience by employing a question that needs to be answered. However, the question may or may not be resolved by the end of the story. Sometimes the storyteller chooses not to resolve the story in order to keep the audience thinking about it.
3. *Emotional content*: Emotion enhances knowledge and understanding. Emotion is part of the human experience that the audience can identify with and relate to.
4. *The gift of your voice*: If the storyteller narrates the story, his or her own voice helps to personalize the story, giving the audience something more meaningful and more engaging than what written words alone can supply. Inflections in the storyteller's voice also help provide the emotional content.
5. *The power of the soundtrack*: Music and sound effects can add another layer of meaning to your story and support and embellish the story. Just make sure your soundtrack complements the story and does not distract the audience. (Suggestion: use instrumental music rather than vocal songs, unless the song itself is the basis of the story.)
6. *Pacing*: Pacing describes the rhythm of the story and how slowly or quickly it progresses. The audience needs time to absorb and process the information in the story. Just as a carefully placed pause is important in the oral telling of a story, a brief break or fading to black can be important in a digital story.
7. *Economy*: Use just enough content to tell the story without overloading the viewer. If a picture really is worth a thousand words, then let a few carefully chosen images help you tell the story. Sometimes you don't have to say something verbally if the picture says it for you, and sometimes you don't need to show an image if your words are conveying your message.

There are two important reasons for such a long and detailed discussion about digital storytelling in this chapter. The first is that if you look at some examples of digital storytelling, you will quickly realize how easy it is to create a digital story without the time-consuming process of learning to use complex video software that sometimes has a steep learning curve. There are many simple programs available for building digital stories quickly and painlessly, allowing you to easily create digital stories for an online or hybrid class. Your digital stories don't even need to include narration; they can simply be text and images.

The second reason for this discussion about digital stories is to encourage you to consider having your students create their own digital stories. Storytelling is an important skill that will help your students in their careers and daily lives. Creating digital stories helps them practice and improve their storytelling skills. It leads to the production of something meaningful that lasts past the end of the school year and can be shared with others. It also makes for a great capstone project in your class. (Chapter 9 is devoted to empowering students to tell their own stories.)

But what this chapter does not include are suggestions for what software to use or detailed instructions on how to create digital or video stories. Why? Quite simply, it is because the technology and the software change too quickly. The world's favorite software for creating video and digital stories might get bought up by a competing company tomorrow or may be replaced by a new version with new bells and whistles.

But even though the technology changes, and even though the software changes, effective and engaging storytelling will never change. The truths and suggestions for great storytelling presented in this book will never be out of date or go out of style.

So how do you find out about the best and/or easiest software to use for creating digital and video stories? Start by asking your peers. Someone at your school or in your district is probably already an expert. Ask around, and you will likely be directed to the creative "techie" types very quickly. Tell them exactly what you are looking for. Do you want software that is cheap or even free? (There are many free web-based programs and apps that you can use to quickly create stories.) Do you want software that is easy, with no learning curve? Do you want big and powerful software?

Also, be sure to tell your mentor specifically what you want the final product to be. Do you want to create a video that you can upload to YouTube? Do you want to create a file that you can embed in your school's learning management system? Do you want software or an app that any and all of your students can use quickly and easily, without getting bogged down in the technical aspects?

Speaking of your students, you might try asking them as well. Some of your students are extremely tech-savvy and already make videos of their own. These students may already have great storytelling skills without even thinking of themselves as storytellers. Learn from them, and get them to help you find the software and tech supplies that you need.

In fact, partnering with your students in this way teaches a great lesson on the value of collaboration. Their strengths are in the use of the software and the technology. Your strengths are in content knowledge and your skills as a storyteller. Collaborate with your students, and you will be modeling some of the most important skills that they will need in their careers.

As stated above, even though the technology changes, effective and engaging storytelling will never change. Again, all of the truths and suggestions for great storytelling presented in this book will never be out of date or go out of style. If you spend time creating a digital story and then decide that you should have used a different format or want to try a different software package, you will have "wasted" very little time. Well-told stories are easily transferable.

For example, stories that you tell in a traditional classroom can easily be converted into text and images on a web page for a hybrid or online class, because you already know how to tell the story. A story you created in text and images can easily be remade into a digital story with narration and images. A digital story you created can easily be remade into a video story. But don't forget: A great story in any format is still a great story. If your engaging and compelling story is composed simply of text and images, there is no reason that it needs to be remade into a digital or video story—unless converting it is something you really want to do.

There is one more point to make in this chapter, and it has to do with narrating your own digital and video stories. Remember truth 1 (and truth 12) from chapter 3? You are well on your way to becoming a great storyteller, so you should never have any reservations about recording your own voice for a digital or video story. Iwancio (2010) explains it quite simply: Recording your own voice can be a difficult part of the process, as many people don't like to hear the sound of their own voice. But your voice is a great gift, and your audience will appreciate it when you share it.

KEY POINTS FROM CHAPTER 7

- Video is a great way to tell stories because you can use so many tools in a video story, such as narration, action footage, special effects, and music. However, an engaging story told orally is always more compelling than a boring video story, even when the video uses all the bells and whistles.
- Digital storytelling can make use of a wide variety of tools, and the resulting story is usually somewhere on a continuum between an oral story and a video with all the special effects.
- Digital stories are easy to create, and easy to embed into online course materials and social media.
- For both video and digital storytelling, you can probably find a coworker, an IT specialist, or even a student who can help you with suggestions on the best software for your project.

Chapter Eight

Photographs That Tell Stories

They say that a picture is worth a thousand words. In fact, a single image can sometimes tell a story more impactfully than any other medium can tell it. Better yet, combine that image with some text, or a storyteller's voice, and you can end up with an extremely powerful story that can change the course of history.

Images have always been important for conveying a narrative. Throughout most of human history, those images had to be created as paintings. However, one may question the accuracy of many famous paintings, as the artist might have taken some liberties with the story. And often the paintings were created many years after the event they depict.

FAMOUS PAINTINGS THAT TELL A STORY

Many famous paintings tell stories that are an important part of human culture. For example, consider *The Last Supper*, painted by Leonardo da Vinci in the 1490s, several hundred years after the event. How accurately are Jesus and the apostles depicted in the painting? Did they really all sit on the same side of the table at this meal? Yet this is the image that comes to mind when most people think of that event in Jesus's life.

Another famous painting is *Washington Crossing the Delaware*, the 1851 painting by Emanuel Leutze. Leutze wasn't present for the actual event, which occurred on the night of December 25–26, 1776, during the American Revolutionary War. How accurate is the painting? It certainly portrays General Washington in a heroic pose, but many historians agree that such a small boat could have easily capsized on that stormy night if Washington had indeed been standing. Yet this is one of the indelible images that tell the story of our nation's independence.

Things changed in the 1800s as photographic techniques were developed, and by the latter half of the 19th century, many of the world's important people and events were being captured in photographs. Although it was difficult and expensive to reproduce these early photographs in books in the 1800s, at least woodcuts, engravings, drawings, and paintings that appeared in books could be based on photographs of actual events. By the early 1900s, photography was becoming commonplace, and it ushered in a new era of storytelling.

FAMOUS PHOTOGRAPHS THAT TELL A STORY

Certain photographs were instrumental in changing cultural perceptions and attitudes and sometimes changing the very fabric of society. Although the photographs discussed here are not reproduced in this book, they are all easy to find on the Internet. Let's start with *Migrant Mother*, a 1936 photograph taken in California by Dorothea Lange. The photo is of a destitute woman and two of her seven children, and the pained expression on the woman's face reflects the difficulties of the times. Indeed, the photo became one of the defining images of the Great Depression.

In addition to the story told by the photo, there is also a story behind the photo as well. The name of the woman in the photo remained a mystery for many years, as Lange hadn't asked her subject's name when the photo was taken. In the 1970s, a reporter tracked down the woman, named Florence Owens. Owens was very critical of Lange, who had passed away in 1965. Owens claimed that she felt exploited by the photo, saying she had never made any money from the use of her image. Indeed, even after Owens passed away, a print of the photograph signed by Lange sold for over $200,000 at an auction in 1998 (Nix, 2014).

Another important photograph is *Raising the Flag on Iwo Jima*, taken in 1945 by Joe Rosenthal. The photo shows five marines and a navy corpsman raising a US flag on the island. The battle for Iwo Jima was particularly bloody, with a staggering number of casualties. This photo of the flag being raised became symbolic of the American successes and ultimate victory over Japan in WWII. It became the basis for the Marine Corps War Memorial in Virginia.

Again, there is a story behind the photo. This photograph actually records the second flag raising on the island, not the first. Earlier in the day, a small flag was raised, but the event was not photographed. Ninety minutes later, an order came through to raise a much larger flag and to capture the moment in a photograph. Over the years, many people have been critical of the photograph, saying it was staged. Also, not all of the men who raised the first flag were part of the effort to raise the second flag, leading to confusion about who is actually shown in the photo.

After the memorial was created, there was even more criticism, especially related to the number of hands and legs in the statue. Since the three-dimensional statue was patterned after the two-dimensional photograph, such criticism is not surprising. But despite such objections, this image remains one of the most important photographs that tell the story of WWII (Lucas, 2013).

Let's look at a few other famous photographs. The 1963 photo of three-year-old John F. Kennedy Jr. saluting the casket of his father, an image captured by photographer Dan Farrell, reflected the mood of the nation and its sense of loss after JFK's assassination. A young Vietnamese girl screaming and running naked down the street after a napalm attack was captured in a photo, *The Terror of War*, by Huynh Cong (Nick) Ut. This photo, sometimes referred to as "Napalm Girl," was taken on June 8, 1972, and helped turn the tide of public opinion about the war in Vietnam.

The publication of the "Napalm Girl" photo also changed the rules for many media outlets who realized the photo was too important not to publish, despite the nudity. Similarly, other famous images changed the rules for publishing photographs that depicted violence. Photographer Eddie Adams snapped a picture of a Vietnamese man in Saigon one second before the man was executed with a bullet to the head. The expression on the victim's face, combined with the casual nature of the execution, horrified viewers around the world when *Saigon Execution* was published.

The use of photos like these to tell stories is just as important today as it has been in the past. Even though today's world is filled with video, and even though most people carry a video camera in the form of a smartphone, taking videos everywhere they go, a simple photograph can still have a huge impact on society. Such photos become the covers of magazines and appear on the front pages of newspapers around the world. The images can redirect public opinion, and help bring about sweeping changes in attitudes and policies. In many cases, a photo that tells a story is worth far more than just a thousand words.

MEMES

The use of photos to tell stories has morphed into something now very popular with today's students: memes. What is a meme? Merriam-Webster defines *meme* as "an idea, behavior, style, or usage that spreads from person to person within a culture" ("Meme," 2018). Many authors have pointed out that humans as a species really aren't very innovative—a few people create something new, and then everyone else copies those ideas. So you could think of a meme as a novel idea that is spread around for everyone else to copy.

Not only are these ideas copied but memes are often modified before they are passed along to other people. As a result, humans are constantly learning about new ideas, adding to and modifying those ideas, and sharing the revised versions with others. Memes may include ideas that change the world in a big way (like the adoption of cars and the suburban lifestyle over the last century), in smaller ways (like the use of zippers instead of buttons or hooks in clothing, or putting wheels on suitcases), or simply with regard to entertainment (like jokes and cartoons).

INTERNET MEMES TELL STORIES

In today's Internet and social media culture, memes can be posted by anyone and shared quickly around the entire world. Internet and social media memes come in a variety of forms, such as a video or animated gif, and with or without text or audio, but the most common form of a meme is simply an image with some text. Therefore, the image becomes the core of the meme and is intended to tell a story—a story that may need a little text to explain it.

If you are not familiar with Internet memes, just try a quick Internet search for "popular internet meme," and click on "images." What you will find is what many of your students see, share, and laugh at every day. Scroll through the images, and you will notice that several of the Internet memes have the same picture but have different text. That's the beauty of an Internet meme—anyone can take an idea that someone else created, make some modifications, and repost it. Then others who enjoy memes will instantly recognize it and understand it.

If the story told by an Internet or social media meme engages the audience and resonates with people, then the meme will be passed along. If the level of engagement is high enough, the meme will often be modified while still retaining enough of the original idea so that people will recognize it as derivative of the original. Sometimes, a meme resonates so strongly that the meme can have a lifespan of several years, with constant modification and evolution.

For the meme to engage, resonate, and survive for very long, the image must tell a story that the audience understands and can relate to. It must convey some type of emotion that everyone can recognize, such as pain, pleasure, sadness, or humor. Although the example in the meme's image may represent a specific event or time, the underlying message of the meme must be timeless if the meme is to survive for very long. And for the meme to have a timeless message, the story told by the image must be easily and quickly discernible. Attention spans are generally too short for memes to survive if viewers can't immediately relate to them.

HOW TO TELL A STORY WITH A PHOTOGRAPH

How do you tell a story with a photograph? Just ask professional photographers! For example, Darren Rowse (2010) gives the following suggestions in his article, "Telling Stories With Photos." First of all, a photograph, just like a story, has the ability to convey emotion, mood, narrative ideas, and messages. The trick is knowing how to capture these characteristics in a photo.

Although you may assume that a photo must be carefully planned in order to capture these traits, that is not always the case. Photos like two that were described above, JFK Jr. saluting his father's casket and "Napalm Girl," were simply the result of an experienced photographer reacting instantly to an important opportunity. Put yourself in the shoes of a professional newspaper or magazine photographer for a moment—imagine carrying a camera all the time, ready to point, focus, and shoot at a moment's notice. It is a combination of luck and experience.

Rowse (2010) goes on to describe other important attributes. First of all, there must be something in the photo that instantly grabs the audience and contains a focal point that leads the viewer into the photo. Sometimes a good photo leaves the viewer wondering what is going on and encourages the viewer to spend more time looking at the photo. Sometimes it is better to include more people in the picture, so that the viewer can see the relationship between the people in the photo. On the other hand, leaving other people out of the photo creates more intrigue, since the viewer wonders who the person in the picture is interacting with.

According to Rowse (2010), the context—or lack thereof—in the picture also helps shape the story. If the viewer is intrigued and looks at every detail in the photo, then the various elements in the photo, or even things in the background of the photo, can provide some context. On the other hand, too many elements or really obvious elements can make the photograph seem clichéd and cause the viewer to lose interest. In contrast, a lack of context can be intentional on the part of the photographer as a way of increasing the viewer's curiosity.

Another photographer, Lindsay Ross (2015), describes the importance of including moments of conflict, learning, action, or struggle in a photo if that photo is going to tell a story. In fact, Ross encourages always resisting the urge to have the subject smile or look at the camera because this can change the focus or emotion of the subject. It is always better to catch a person "in the act" and "in the moment" so that the subject's emotions and expressions are natural and real.

Ross (2015) provides some additional suggestions, including taking multiple shots from different angles. Good photography is as much about the editing process as the picture-taking process, so shoot from many angles and decide later which is the best shot. Also, make sure that there are some details in the photos that help tell the story. For example, something as simple as a child's dirty feet can be an important detail that helps tell the story.

Ross (2015) goes on to describe advice from fellow photographer Chris Jones. Jones's son Mitchell died when he was only 10 years old, and Jones had this to say about taking photos: "I began taking photos long before Mitchell's diagnosis, but upon learning his life would be cut short, I began to see moments differently. I stopped taking photos of what things looked like and focused more on capturing what life felt like."

TEACHERS USING PHOTOGRAPHS TO TELL STORIES

How can you use photos to tell a story to your students? First of all, if you have been telling stories orally or using digital or video stories, then using a photo to tell a story is a nice change of pace and adds a new dimension to your curriculum and your teaching style. In a traditional classroom or in an online environment, a photo that tells a story is a great way to engage your audience, start a discussion, and prompt students to use their critical-thinking skills.

For example, in a traditional classroom, show a photograph projected on a screen, and let the photo speak for itself. Say nothing for 15 or 30 seconds or even longer, and give your students a chance to take it in and think about what they see. Then you can provide some background or explanation as needed, and use the photo as a lead-in to a longer story, a lesson, an assignment, or a discussion. You can also do the same in an online class, using a single photo to start a conversation or a lesson.

Once you are comfortable finding and using photos to tell a story, you are ready to take your own storytelling photos. You don't need a fancy camera or years of photography experience. It is not about taking a perfect picture. Rather, it is about capturing a moment that tells a story.

KEY POINTS FROM CHAPTER 8

- Before photography, paintings were the best way to create an image to tell a story. However, paintings did not always accurately portray the people or the events. The use of photography has changed the way stories are told.

- There are many famous photographs that tell a story that most people instantly recognize. Many of these photographs were instrumental in changing public opinion and providing a call to action.
- Internet memes are popular with many of your students and offer another way to use photographs to tell stories.
- There are many ways to use photographs to tell stories when you teach, including using a photograph to set the scene for the story or to start a class discussion.
- A fancy camera is not required for taking a photo that tells a story. The camera in your smartphone is more than adequate.

Chapter Nine

Empowering Students to Tell Their Own Stories

When teachers tell stories, students are engaged. When students get the opportunity to tell their own stories, they become even more engaged and take a bigger role in their own learning. In fact, there are many benefits to encouraging students to tell their own stories.

1. Students will learn to find their voice.

Most, if not all, people want to find ways to tell their stories, and your students are no exception: They love to tell stories. If you have ever been in a classroom of 30 elementary school kids, you know that there are at least 150 stories just waiting to be told. Unfortunately, most kids of that age are not yet expert storytellers, and their stories generally ramble on without direction. But since storytelling is such an important skill, you will be helping your students immensely by showing them how to find their voice and fine-tune their stories.

It is not just the elementary students who need to improve their storytelling skills. Unless your students are taking journalism, acting, or theater classes, they might not be getting any training in storytelling. No matter what subject area you teach, there are always ways to integrate storytelling into your curriculum and your assignments. When you give students the opportunity to tell their stories, you will find that they are much more excited about learning and more engaged in the content.

2. Students can relate their personal stories to concepts from your class.

You want your students to find application and relevance in what they learn, and that is why stories told by you, the teacher, are so effective. But even more powerful is the learning that occurs when students demonstrate their understanding by relating concepts from your class to their own stories. When students tell personal stories directly related to content in your class, they are demonstrating critical-thinking skills, as described in chapter 6.

There is another advantage to students telling their own stories—stories told by students can be extremely meaningful to other students. There will always be a subset of students who listen to their peers more than they listen to teachers. Allowing students to tell their stories can literally put them in the role of the teacher, providing even more connections between core concepts and applications.

3. Stories connect people and improve conversations.

The telling of stories connects student to teacher, and student to student, and it improves and expands conversations. LaGarde (2016) describes her experience teaching young students how to write. She had been frustrated with her students' editing and revising of their papers, so she began having them read their papers aloud, hoping it would help her students catch their own mistakes. As they read their papers, LaGarde would often stop them to ask them about their writing processes and why they wrote what they wrote.

LaGarde quickly realized that when students answered her questions, she was actually hearing many of her students' voices for the first time. She described the impact it had on her and her teaching: "I'd gotten to know their data, but I'd neglected getting to know them as learners or people. In short, I knew their statistics, but I didn't know their stories" (LaGarde, 2016). She then began assigning more and more projects that gave students opportunities to tell their own stories.

LaGarde's insights on these new conversations with her students are powerful: "When we know our students' stories, we're able to move from simply knowing how our students perform to understanding why they perform that way. When we learn our students' stories, we're able to move beyond simply doing what works for most students to customizing learning for individual needs. And when we know our students' stories, we are able to move from merely being invested in our students' success to being invested in them as people" (LaGarde, 2016).

4. Having students tell their stories can provide different points of view.

In addition to connecting students and expanding conversations, student storytellers can provide other points of view to their peers and their teachers. Abamu (2018) describes what happened when high school students took the stage at the Kennedy Center in Washington, DC, to tell their versions of stories from history. One student, Janelle Lott, read a poem she had written from the perspective of Madison Hemings, one of the children born to Sally Hemings, a slave who belonged to Thomas Jefferson.

Janelle's poem was a passionate story, and an angry story, of what it was like to fall through the cracks of history: "I will no longer allow his legacy to silence me. My father who owned me and my family as slaves, mentioned as nothing more than mere apprentices in his will" (Abamu, 2018). It turned out that the poem was a reflection of Janelle's own situation. In Janelle's words, "I recently just came back in contact with my father, and I took all the anger and placed it into my poem" (Abamu, 2018).

To the other students in the audience, Janelle's story was a powerful one that gave a different point of view from what one might find in a history book. Janelle and her peers felt empowered by the opportunity to tell stories. In fact, Janelle said it was the first time in her entire school experience that she had been able to express her feelings creatively in class, and the first time she had been able to share those feelings in a safe way with peers.

5. Students can make better decisions when they hear the stories of other students.

Everyone can benefit from hearing the stories of others, and again, your students are no exception. For example, students can make decisions about where to go to college by reading the stories of other students. Mock (2011) describes an initiative by Duke University to share student stories with incoming students. To accomplish this, the dean of undergraduate admissions recruited several current students to blog on the Duke website about their experiences.

The bloggers came from a variety of backgrounds, majors, and class levels. The student pool also included an international student and a student who had studied abroad. They blogged about everything from move-in day to campus life to choosing classes. Because the stories were told by students and were authentic, they were much more useful to prospective students than college brochures and other advertising. The experience benefited the bloggers as well, giving them an opportunity to improve their storytelling skills (Mock, 2011).

6. Storytelling is an important skill.

Storytelling is an important skill for your students' entire professional and personal lives. For example, high school and college students who have storytelling skills can write better application essays for college and graduate school. Lang (2012) describes what happened after he read his own daughter's AP literature paper about the challenges of running a half marathon. The paper started out well, with "rich imagery and descriptive details, just the kind of thing a writing teacher wants to see."

However, the final paragraph was similar to many of the papers that Lang's students typically write, with a very predictable ending: "The experience had taught her to reach for her dreams, that the sky was the limit, that anything was possible if she worked hard enough, etc." (Lang, 2012). Had he not already read hundreds of essays that all sounded the same, he might have congratulated his daughter on a great job. Instead, he recognized the tired and clichéd ending of her story.

After this experience, and after reading a few more college application letters from his students, Lang set out to discover exactly what colleges are looking for in a personal application essay. He was surprised to find out there are three key points that college selection committees are looking for, and unfortunately, most students only manage to address one or two of these points at best.

The first point is for students to tell their story with an eye to the opportunity they are seeking (Lang, 2012). Some students do a good job of telling their own story, but many students simply make a list of their accomplishments. Given that committees will only spend a matter of minutes on each application, a long list of accomplishments, even when tied to a long narrative, doesn't hold the committee's attention. In a stack of applications from "high achievers," a personal story needs to focus on the most important character traits that set each student apart.

The second point is that applicants must articulate a vision of their future (Lang, 2012). Most students think this means providing a time line for accomplishing tasks, such as graduation and employment. Instead, committees are looking for an explanation of very tangible long-term goals, and how this particular college opportunity will help the students reach those goals.

The third point is for applicants to show how this particular college opportunity will connect past achievements to future goals (Lang, 2012). This is where very few applications shine. Selection committees know that the colleges they represent cannot admit or help all students, and they want to make sure that their program is indeed a good fit for the students who are accepted.

This is where masterful storytelling is really important. The student who tells a unique and engaging story, ties an important experience to a long-term vision, and explains how college will become part of this story is the student who will be accepted into an elite college or graduate program. Preparing your students to become expert storytellers can help ensure their success years down the road.

Beyer (2014) offers another suggestion when preparing students to become storytellers. She notes that even when students are trained in storytelling in majors like public communication, film, and journalism, many still fall short when telling their own stories. Many students have not reflected on their own strengths and weaknesses or are simply very uncomfortable doing so and therefore cannot tell their own story in a compelling way that will resonate with their audience. Beyer's recommendation: reflect, practice, and develop confidence when applying storytelling skills to one's own narrative.

7. Telling personal stories can be healing.

Louise DeSalvo has written an excellent and well-researched book titled *Writing as a Way of Healing: How Telling Our Stories Transforms Our Lives* (1999). As a college English professor, she has had years of experience coaching students on how to write about their challenges and how these challenges have affected them emotionally. DeSalvo also talks about how her writing has been therapeutic in dealing with her own struggles.

At some point in our lives, we all have to deal with challenges and struggles. You may think you know your students well, but all of them have likely encountered problems and events that have shaped their lives in ways they don't often discuss with their teachers. And the older your students are, the more life experiences they have endured. Everyone deals with the aftermath of challenges in different ways, including therapy, substance abuse, or through dangerous behavior. As DeSalvo suggests, writing about personal stories may be the best and safest method of coping.

DeSalvo (1999) describes a study in which a large number of students were divided into four groups. One group wrote about trivial topics, such as a description of their living room. The second group wrote about traumatic experiences—but only the facts of those experiences. The third group wrote only to vent their emotions without details of the events that brought the emotions about. The fourth group wrote about both traumatic events and the associated emotions.

Not surprisingly, the study stirred up the strongest negative feelings in the fourth group, students who wrote about both events and emotions. At first, the facilitators of the study were concerned that perhaps the writing activities had done more harm than good. But four months later, the students in the fourth group reported that their spirits had improved significantly, they felt some of their issues had been resolved, and they had a more positive outlook.

But the facilitators weren't convinced by the students' self-reporting alone, so they collected empirical data as well. They had noted that, prior to the writing activity, all of the students visited the campus health center at the same rate. Six months after the writing activity, the first three groups were still vising the health center at the same rate. However, the fourth group—students who wrote about both events and emotions—had reduced their visits to the health center by 50%. Since this study was published, many experiments have shown similar results for students describing events in their lives and how they felt about those events—an improved outlook on life and fewer health problems.

There are many examples in the news of how writing personal stories about traumatic events and emotions helps those who have experienced tragedy. Shammas (2018) describes how students at Marjory Stoneman Douglas

High School in Parkland, Florida, have written their personal stories to deal with the trauma they experienced after the mass shooting in February 2018.

In a similar vein, Kelleher (2016) describes how undocumented students known as "DREAMers" (immigrants who meet the requirements of the Development, Relief, and Education for Alien Minors Act) have written about their experiences. Telling their personal stories has been therapeutic and healing for many of these kids. As one student said, "People are telling me my story before I get out my story"—that is, people were doing so until she began insisting that reporters dig more deeply into the experiences of DREAMers before publishing their articles.

In summary, the benefits are many.

There are numerous benefits to encouraging your students to tell their own stories. Some of the benefits are seen immediately, such as when personal stories are related to important concepts in your course. Some of the benefits will help in a few months or a few years, such as when storytelling skills improve one's chances of getting into college or graduate school. And some of the benefits last a lifetime, as when people tell their stories to cope with challenges and trauma. Indeed, helping your students improve their storytelling skills can literally help them be happy for their entire life.

HELPING STUDENTS TELL THEIR STORIES

How do you help students tell their stories? First of all, never forget that the emphasis should be on the story itself instead of on the technology used for or the method of telling the story. A story that resonates will resonate no matter what technology is used. On the other hand, a story that doesn't engage the audience won't resonate even if all possible high-tech bells and whistles are in place. Therefore, when you assign a storytelling activity for your students, focus on the characteristics of good stories (the truths described in chapter 3) before you focus on the medium to be used.

In fact, you may want to start explaining the characteristics of good stories at the beginning of the school year or semester. As a teacher who tells stories, you can then begin modeling effective storytelling early on, and your students will recognize those characteristics in all the stories you tell. Or perhaps you will decide to tell a few stories first and then describe their characteristics.

The advantage to explaining storytelling truths early on is that students can see those characteristics in the stories you tell from the beginning. However, you may feel a bit self-conscious (at first) and think that your students will be critiquing you with every story you tell, so use whichever approach feels right to you. And don't worry so much about your students critiquing your stories; just explain to them that they will soon be telling their own stories, and you will be critiquing them.

Heick (2017) describes several steps for helping students tell their stories through social media. These steps focus first on the story and not on the delivery platform. The initial steps include having a story to tell, having an "audience-first" mentality, and providing examples of excellent storytelling on which to model their stories. Heick's final step is this: After considering all the other steps, use social media to share the story. In closing, Heick suggests helping students understand that it is all about why they should tell digital stories and not how they should tell them.

KEY POINTS FROM CHAPTER 9

There are numerous benefits to empowering students to tell their own stories, such as the following:

- Students love to tell stories, and they can find their voice and become more engaged in learning when they assume the role of storyteller.
- Students can relate their personal stories to concepts in class, demonstrating critical-thinking skills.
- Stories help connect student to student, and student to teacher, and they improve conversations in your classroom.
- When students tell stories, they can shape those stories to provide different points of view.
- Some students find stories told by other students even more engaging than stories told by teachers.
- Helping your students to become great storytellers provides them with an important skill that will help them in their careers and their lives.
- Telling personal stories can be healing. Many of your students have been through challenging or even traumatic events, and telling their personal stories can be excellent therapy.

Chapter Ten

Storytelling for Staff and Administrators

So you are an administrator or a staff member and not a teacher? You are still reading the right book! The title of this book is *Imperative Narratives: Storytelling Secrets for Teachers, Staff, and Administrators*, not *Imperative Narratives Just for Teachers*. Telling the right stories and changing the narrative is just as crucial for you as it is for teachers. In fact, changing the narrative of your school may be even more important than telling stories in the classroom.

SCHOOLS COMPARED TO BUSINESSES

Here is a question that may surprise some readers and generate some strong opinions: Should a school be run like a business? Don't worry; that is not a question to be answered in this book! But there are some aspects of a school that are very similar to those of a business. You want a healthy organizational climate at your school, there are economic decisions to be made, there are customers you want to make happy, and you want to be in good standing in the community.

Therefore, just as in a business, the stories that the employees tell within the organization, the stories that you tell to the community, and the stories that the community hears and shares about your school, are all crucial.

How crucial are these stories? Let's start with some examples of businesses that told the wrong stories. Many of these examples are discussed in college-level marketing classes across the country as case studies of what not to do. In 1985, Coca-Cola changed its formula, and introduced "New Coke." This change, without the input of brand-loyal soda drinkers, was interpreted by many as Coca-Cola saying that it didn't care what customers thought. The negative reaction by consumers hurt the company's profits for a decade.

Coke's main competitor, Pepsi, also got its story wrong in a 2017 commercial featuring Kendall Jenner. The intention was to copy the feel-good approach that Coca-Cola had used in the 1970s and show that sharing a soft drink can bring people together. Unfortunately, the story told in the commercial was seen as an insensitive commentary on the Black Lives Matter movement. Even though the ad was pulled after only one day, the damage was already done. Pepsi spent far more money on apologies and trying to change its story than it had paid for the original, high-priced ad.

In 2017, the confectioner Cadbury dropped "Easter" from the front of the packaging on its chocolate eggs and bunnies. Many customers got irate because they felt Cadbury was saying that the holiday didn't matter to a company that sells more eggs and bunnies at Easter than any other time of the year. IHOP (International House of Pancakes) made a big mistake when the company tweeted that its pancakes were "flat but have a great personality," a story that offended many female customers.

Budweiser made a major faux pas by adding the statement, "The perfect beer for removing 'no' from your vocabulary for the night—#upforwhatever" to its products, a marketing gimmick that offended many customers who felt that the marketing approach made light of the problem of date rape. Apparently marketing employees at Budweiser did not think through the implications of the story they were telling until the products were already on store shelves.

In each of these cases, the businesses made marketing decisions that they later regretted. Instead of telling stories that showed that they cared about customers, they told stories that were insensitive or just plain inappropriate. These companies also found out the hard way that telling a new story to bring back customers is very expensive and time consuming. Having to change the narrative is about much more than just dealing with a short-term dip in profits—it is about rebuilding trust over the long haul.

These stories about businesses are "external" stories—stories that people outside the companies hear and share. But businesses also have "internal" stories, told by the employees. These internal stories create the culture and climate in the workplace and can have a huge impact on the success of the business. When the stories told within the company are positive, employees are productive and take pride in their work. When the stories are negative, the entire company suffers.

Like a business, your school has external stories that affect how the community views your school. If those stories are negative, the community loses faith and trust in the school, the school's mission, and sometimes even the school's employees. Also like a business, your school has internal stories—told by the employees—that create the school's climate and culture.

Positive stories mean employees are happy, take pride in their work, and stay employed at the school for a longer time. Negative stories destroy morale and lead to high turnover.

A BRIEF ASIDE ABOUT "LEADERSHIP"

When people think of leadership at a school, they are usually envisioning the roles of the people at the top of the organizational structure: superintendents, principals, presidents, and chancellors. Ideally, these leaders should also be the chief storytellers of your school. After all, these leaders are tasked with creating and maintaining the culture and mission of the school, and since the narrative is so important in making this happen, these leaders should be skilled at telling stories.

However, the reality is that not just some but all of the employees at the school are storytellers. Whether the employees are administrators, support staff, or teachers, they are all telling stories every day to other employees, to students, and to members of the community. Therefore, from this point forward, you must think of yourself as a leader at your school, whether you have the highest paid—or the lowest paid—position there. No matter your job description, you are a leader and a storyteller at your school. Just accept the role!

CHANGING THE INTERNAL STORIES AT YOUR SCHOOL

Almost everyone has toiled in an unhealthy work environment at some point. Perhaps you had a rude manager at your fast-food job in high school. Perhaps you had an inflexible boss when you were a student assistant in college. Perhaps in your current job as a teacher, you don't see eye to eye with administration. An unhealthy work environment drags everyone down. It creates an unhappy climate and culture in the workplace, which in turn destroys morale. Once an unhealthy work environment exists, it can continue to spiral out of control until someone like you steps in to help make a change.

How and why does a bad situation continue to get worse? It is perpetuated by the stories that employees tell. As this book has been emphasizing since the beginning, stories are all about emotions and feelings, not facts and data. Positive stories bring about positive emotions. Negative stories bring about negative emotions. Therefore, if your school's climate is a negative one and is made worse by negative stories, it is your job as a school leader to help change the narrative.

To maintain a positive narrative and a healthy environment, it is crucial for everyone in the school to understand the organization's values and mission. All schools, like all large businesses, go through cycles—new leadership, new employees, and new challenges. Even in a school with a positive and successful past, employees leave and new employees come aboard. Sometimes the organization as a whole forgets its past and loses sight of its values and mission. You can help right the ship.

But righting the ship is not always easy. One person can make a difference, but doing so can be hard work and take time. Like all social movements, change starts slowly, but it can snowball as more people see the value in making a change. Regardless of your leadership position—at the top or the bottom of the organizational structure—you can help recapture the school's values, find stories that reflect the school's mission, and share stories that reflect those values and mission.

There are several books available on organizational storytelling. Although these books are not focused on schools, good organizational storytelling practices can work within any organization. Kate Marek, for example, describes the process of building stories within a library setting, but the same steps work within a school setting. She lists three important questions to answer as the stories are collected, listed here with the emphasis changed to describe schools (Marek, 2011):

1. *What are five to ten pivotal events in your organization's history?* These stories might be about buildings, awards, expansions, renovations, or other seminal events in your school's past. Unfortunately, as employees leave and new people come on board, it is easy to forget about these events. Find people who remember these stories, or at least find documents that reflect these events, and breathe some life back into these stories.
2. *Who are your school's heroes?* These might be the founders of your school, or they might be important people from the school's past, including administrators, staff, teachers, former students, or even community members who contributed to making your school great. Unfortunately, the stories about these people may have been lost, replaced with only names on plaques. Again, find people who remember these stories, so you can tell them again.
3. *What key values or characteristics of your school are highlighted in your stories?* Think about your school's strengths and what you currently do well at your school. Think about what you did well in the past that should be made a priority once again. What stories from the past relate to the school's mission statements? What stories relate to the school's vision for the future?

Marek also makes a critical observation when it comes to these stories—you must make sure they are accurate! Stories can morph over time like a game of telephone. She gives an example of how Al Gore was burned by inaccuracy during his 2000 presidential campaign, after telling the story of a girl in an overcrowded Florida classroom. Unfortunately, he got some of the details wrong, and the mistake was enough to discredit his entire message about education, "causing subsequent collateral damage way beyond the lost potential of that single story" (Marek, 2011).

Stephen Denning has also written extensively about organizational storytelling based on his experience as a director with the World Bank. He recommends building a catalog of stories for the organization that can be used for the following purposes (Denning, 2004):

- *to spark action*—stories that show your audience the need for change;
- *to communicate who you are*—stories that build trust and explain your views;
- *to transmit values*—stories that describe where you have come from and where you are headed;
- *to foster collaboration*—stories that describe how the narrative is shared within the organization;
- *to tame the grapevine*—stories (often humorous) that are designed to be passed from one employee to another in a positive way;
- *to share knowledge*—stories that contain important facts and messages that can be passed along throughout the organization; and
- *to lead people into the future*—stories that are accurate yet general enough to not turn out to be wrong, related to the vision of the organization.

Annette Simmons is another expert on organizational storytelling. She has described six kinds of stories that every organization needs—and indeed, that every individual needs—to have at the ready (2006):

1. *"Who I am" stories*, communicating who you are and helping build trust;
2. *"Why I am here" stories*, explaining your motivations;
3. *"The vision" stories*, helping recruit listeners to join a cause;
4. *"Teaching" stories*, explaining what you want the audience to know and how things should be done;
5. *"Values-in-action" stories*, inspiring the audience toward action without telling the audience what to do; and
6. *"I know what you are thinking" stories*, addressing objections that you predict your audience will have, even before the audience states the objections.

While each of the three authors cited in this section describe organizational storytelling a bit differently, you can see many common threads. When the leaders of your school, including yourself, begin gathering and sharing the recommended stories, the organizational climate in your school will improve. Employees begin to work together as a team, morale improves, and the entire school becomes more effective in meeting the goals of the mission statement.

CHANGING THE EXTERNAL STORIES AT YOUR SCHOOL

Although it can be difficult to change the stories that the community hears and shares about your school, these external stories are just as important as the internal stories. As with the internal stories, employees swap stories with family, friends, students, and others in the community. And just as with the internal stories, all those who share stories with the community should consider themselves to be leaders within the organization.

Problems with the external stories that are told to the community are often blamed on the top leadership and on poor marketing. Indeed, the top leadership should take at least part of the blame when the stories are negative. Unfortunately, many leaders are not expert storytellers, and once a few negative stories get passed along, it is extremely difficult to turn the situation around. Plus, there are often roadblocks from the district level that can make it challenging to tell the right stories.

But leadership must find a way to get the right stories told even with these challenges. As the internal stories improve and sweep through the organization, these same stories will become part of the external narrative that reaches the community. Stick with these same positive stories; use them to build identity and trust both inside and outside of the school. Consider every story to be a marketing tactic even if you are not officially part of the decision-making process for marketing.

In fact, when it comes to marketing, many school leaders feel that they have little say in tactics and implementation, since decisions about marketing—and the budget for marketing—are often overseen at the district level. Feeling that it is your responsibility to market your school while not having a say in the marketing budget or process is an unfortunate position to be in. Even when that is the case, the stories you and the other employees tell can still be a powerful force for change.

If you can become part of the marketing team for your school or district, you will have a great opportunity to select the best external stories to tell, and to share those stories with the community. But what can you do if you are not part of the marketing team? There are still ways you can tell stories, even without a marketing budget, without the costly production of marketing videos, and without fancy press releases.

Today, social media can help level the playing field, making it possible for anyone to share stories for everyone to see. Choose stories carefully, post them on social media, and encourage employees, students (depending on their ages, of course), and their family and friends to follow you. Over time, your number of followers will steadily increase, and you will find that members of the community at large are watching their local school's social media. By telling stories as described by Kate Marek, Stephen Denning, and Annette Simmons, you will be able to promote positive aspects of your school and share your vision and mission.

It is also easier to get coverage on the local television news than you might think. While most organizations send out official press releases about school events and encourage news departments to send out a reporter and photographer, it is often difficult to make everything fall into place that way. But there is a very effective, efficient, and low-cost technique to still get the coverage you want for your school.

An example of this technique was recently used by a college teacher who was helping a local K–12 charter school expand its outdoor classroom and garden area during a Green Apple Day of Service. After initially receiving a press release, the three local news stations showed little interest, citing the difficulty in scheduling a reporter and photographer on a Saturday. So the teacher got creative.

He brought a simple, handheld video camera to the event (even a cell phone would have worked just fine), filmed the kids and parents working, and conducted a few simple interviews with the volunteers. The teacher then posted the video clips (in raw form, not even edited) on YouTube, with each clip as a separate video. He then sent a short email to the three local news stations with a half-page description of the event and links to the video clips. By Sunday evening, one of the stations picked up the story and used the online video clips to put together a three-minute segment that was shown on the evening news.

With minimal effort and no out-of-pocket expenses, the teacher was able to tell the story of the event—even without a professional reporter or photographer on the scene. So many people saw the news segment on TV that members of the community volunteered their time to continue the project, and some even offered cash donations.

This was a low-tech solution that did not require a big marketing department at the school or the services of a reporter, yet it led to a news segment on the exact story that the teacher and the school wanted to share. This is a technique that can be used by anyone at any school—including you!

KEY POINTS FROM CHAPTER 10

- In many ways, your school is like a business. The sharing of negative stories in the workplace damages its organizational climate and lowers morale.

- The sharing of negative stories with the community damages the standing of the school in the community.
- Everyone at your school who tells stories should be considered a school leader—including you.
- You can improve the situation at your school by changing the narrative—by employees telling positive "internal" stories and sharing positive "external" stories with the community.
- Organizational storytelling includes telling stories that spark action, build trust, emphasize values, and foster collaboration.
- There are many ways to get your school's stories told without relying on just press releases and the local news.

Chapter Eleven

Changing the Narrative to Make a Difference

If you have made it this far in the book, then you are already well on your way to becoming a great storyteller and making a big difference in the world by changing narratives. The goals of this chapter are to tie everything together that has been discussed so far and to address the importance of changing your own story.

Step 1: Recognize the Power of Story

In chapter 2, you were given an assignment: Listen to everything in your environment (discussions at work, discussions with friends and family, and what you see, hear, and read in the media), and make a mental note every time you hear the term *story*. By now, you are probably much more aware of how often the term is used and how important stories are in society.

In fact, you have probably come to realize how important stories are in your own life. When you go to a movie theater, binge-watch Netflix, read a novel, watch the evening news, or describe your experiences when you talk to friends and family, you are diving into stories. These stories are important in your professional life and your personal life. They help you learn, keep you entertained, and connect you to the rest of the world. Human brains are literally wired for story.

Step 2: Trust That You Can Become a Great Storyteller

This reflects truth 1—and truth 12—from chapter 3. You now have the tools to become a truly great storyteller. Just follow the rest of the truths in chapter 3. Make your stories compelling, impactful, and memorable, and they will resonate with your audience. Be honest and authentic, and you will build trust with your audience. Keep your stories short, but remember to include the details that your audience wants to hear.

Don't forget that the story of one person can be more powerful than the story of two people, a hundred people, or a million people. Tell stories that appeal to the heart and the gut, and stir people's emotions. Remember that stories will always have a bigger impact than data. Sharing data puts people to sleep. But stories stick with people for life.

Don't forget to practice your stories. Have fun telling them. Be dramatic! Don't sound like a robot. Smile! Talk with your hands. Practice telling stories while driving or in front of a mirror. Practice telling stories to friends and family. Watch other storytellers as they practice their own storytelling skills.

Step 3: Tell the Right Stories

If you are a teacher, tell stories that serve as applications for the concepts you want to teach. If a story isn't a clear example or application of the concept, then it isn't the right story to tell. It doesn't matter whether you teach the concept first and follow with the story or start with the story and then teach the concept. As long as they are tied together, the story will stick and so will the concept.

Don't be afraid to tell personal stories. You may feel uncomfortable at first, but sharing something personal in a story helps build trust with your audience, creates empathy, and helps you connect with students. After hearing your stories, students may then be willing to share personal stories of their own with you; once they do so, you have created a dialogue and a conversation that didn't exist before.

Step 4: Tell the Right Stories at the Right Time

Remember that a story is much more powerful when told in the right context. A story told out of context can be just plain awkward! Notice how the audience responds to your stories, and be ready to respond to your audience appropriately. If you tell a story that makes your audience uncomfortable, make sure you are telling that story for the right reasons. Be aware of who else might be listening when you tell a story. A negative story that falls on the wrong ears may be the story that is quickly shared with everyone.

Step 5: Learn to Tell Stories in a Variety of Modalities

If you are a teacher, you can tell your stories in person while standing in front of a class. You can tell oral stories in an audio podcast. You can tell stories in the form of a digital story or a video. Although telling a story in person can be more impactful than playing a recording, a good story stands on its own and resonates with the audience, regardless of the modality.

Don't forget that photos can also tell stories. A photo that stirs emotions in a single still image can be powerful! If you need to supply details for the story to make sense, start with the photo to grab the viewer's attention, and then follow up with an explanation.

You can also use social media to share stories. Using social media in a consistent way to share positive stories will help you build an audience of followers. The larger your audience, the faster your stories will be shared. Use social media to share "internal" stories in your school. Over time, they will become part of the "external" stories your school shares with the community.

Step 6: Give Students a Chance to Tell Their Own Stories

Empower your students to tell their own stories. When your students can apply the concepts in your course to the stories in their own lives, they are demonstrating critical thinking. When you encourage students to tell stories, you will quickly begin to have deeper and more meaningful conversations with them. Storytelling allows students to find their own voices. Students who find their own voices develop confidence, dream big, and set higher goals for themselves.

When your students learn to become storytellers, you will have given them a powerful tool that will enable them to accomplish much more in life. Students who are storytellers may get into better colleges and graduate programs and find better careers. Students who become master storytellers have the opportunity to change the current narratives of society and make the world a better place.

Learning to be a storyteller can also help students heal their own wounds from the past. Many of your students have been through difficult, even terrible, situations and experiences, and learning to tell those stories can offer more benefit than years of therapy can provide. Students who learn to tell their own stories can literally turn their own lives around.

Step 7: Change the Stories You Tell About Your Students

Many students are held back by the negative stories that previous teachers, staff, and administrators have told about them. Sometimes students don't know about these stories and so don't understand why they have become locked into a path that limits them. Sometimes these negative stories are shared with the students, who then think the stories are true and cannot be changed. When you change the stories you tell about your students, you open up opportunities for them and even change the way they think about themselves.

Step 8: Change the Stories You Tell About Your School

If you are a staff member, administrator, or a teacher, tell the positive stories about your school. Find stories of your school's heroes. Find stories that reflect your school's vision and mission. Find stories that build trust.

Share these stories with the other employees at your school, and then share the stories with others in your community. Remember that when you tell stories about your school, you are a leader at your school.

Step 9: Change the Stories You Tell About Yourself

The most difficult narrative to change may be your own story. Why? To change your story, you must first acknowledge that your story needs changing. It may require that you address the roadblocks that are preventing you from reaching your goals or may even require you to acknowledge your own faults, flaws, and limitations. It is completely natural that human beings don't like to accept their own shortcomings.

Why are bookstores filled with self-help books? It is because so many people are unhappy with their situations. Why are there so many different self-help books, and why do some people buy so many of them? It is because the first self-help book they read may not solve the problem, so they read another, then another, and then another. Why don't self-help books usually solve the problem? It is simply because most of these books don't get to the heart of the problem. They don't help people edit their own stories.

There have been many things in this book described as "truths." But this truth may be the most important one of all: Nothing in your life will change until you change your thinking. Changing your thinking means changing the stories you tell yourself about you and your life. The good news is that once you have changed your stories and therefore changed your thinking, you truly can be happier and more successful.

If you are reading this book, it is because you honestly and deeply care about education. You care about students, and you want them to be successful. You are proud of your job and proud of the work you do. You truly want to make a difference in the world. Otherwise, you wouldn't have picked up this book.

But even the most dedicated teachers, staff, and administrators can get burned out while working in education. Teachers get burned out by behavioral issues, dealing with parents, and dealing with the pressures put on them by administration. Staff get burned out by teachers and administrators and the negative stories they share. Administrators get burned out due to headaches that come from students, parents, teachers, staff, district supervisors, and unhappy community members. On top of that, administrators have to make everyone happy while balancing their budgets. No wonder so many people in education are burned out.

The best way to avoid this burnout is to change the narrative about you and your situation. This may sound trite and superficial, but this process requires much more than just "the power of positive thinking" as described in so many self-help books. This is literally about contemplating the old story about yourself, accepting the shortcomings in that story, throwing out that old story, writing a new story, and then sharing that story with the world. This process is not always easy, and it often takes time. But it can be done, and it is worth the effort.

One of the best and most readable books on the subject is *Redirect: Changing the Stories We Live By*, by Timothy Wilson (2015). Wilson, a psychology professor, has spent three decades looking at the science of changing behavior. He has come to the conclusion that most of our social and governmental programs that are designed to reduce drug and alcohol use, teen pregnancies, and criminal behavior simply don't work because they don't help people change their stories.

In fact, he shows that some of these programs, such as D.A.R.E. (Drug Abuse Resistance Education) and Scared Straight, show little benefit in changing behavior and can even worsen the problems they seek to address. For example, by trying to scare kids with the possible negative outcomes of bad behavior, you can actually plant negative stories into their heads. Several studies have shown that exposure to the Scared Straight program actually leads to a statistically significant increase in criminal behavior. Yet these programs continue to be funded and promoted.

Wilson's solution is to help people turn their negative stories into positive stories, and research shows this approach is indeed far more successful. One of the first examples he discusses in his book is a common example from education. "Meghan" and "Sarah" are college freshmen who just got their first big exam back, and they both failed it. Meghan is stuck in a "pessimism cycle," but Sarah is in an "optimism cycle." With the failing score on her first exam, Meghan says to herself, "I'm a failure, and I can't make it here at college."

With Meghan telling herself that she is a failure, her stress level rises and her level of effort falls. This in turn leads to additional bad grades, which simply reinforces the original narrative of failure. Sarah, on the other hand, tells herself, "I'm fine; I just need to work a little harder and develop better study skills." With this story, Sarah keeps her stress level low, and her level of effort increases. This in turn leads to better grades, which reinforces her narrative of eventual success.

The intervention that is required to get a person back into an optimism cycle can be surprisingly minimal. Wilson cites studies that show that by simply watching a short video of college seniors saying, "I did poorly at first, but I developed better study skills and my grades improved" is enough to prompt many students to try editing their own stories. Once these negative stories are edited into more positive ones, outlook and behavior can begin to change. Eventually, the pessimism cycle is replaced with a cycle of optimism and success.

Another of Wilson's solutions is an ancient one, commonly called "Do good, be good." Many people with risky or criminal behavior act out because they feel disconnected from their community. When people reconnect and get involved in their community again, they begin to edit their personal stories into more positive ones. This in turn changes their thinking and their behaviors. Wilson cites studies that show that when prompting at-risk teens to do volunteer work in their community, there is often a significant reduction in the incidence of bad behavior.

In both of these solutions, the change in outlook and behavior begins with editing personal stories. When the stories are negative, a cycle ensues that traps people. When these stories are tweaked and nudged into something more positive, people get back on track to meet better goals. The change in the story leads to a positive view, which leads to better habits, which leads to an overall change in behavior, which leads to success.

Another insightful book on this topic is *The Power of Story: Change Your Story, Change Your Destiny in Business and in Life*, by Jim Loehr (2007). Loehr, a performance psychologist, has worked with world-class athletes and business executives as well as average people to help them change their narratives to find success. His approach, like that of Wilson, is to alter negative mindsets and thinking patterns by changing the stories people tell about themselves.

According to Loehr, the inner dialogue that people repeat to themselves over and over creates a cause-and-effect loop that has a significant influence on every aspect of life. Editing the personal narrative into a positive story can flip this loop, bring people out of a rut of defeat and depression, and start them onto a path of success. Editing the narrative can begin as soon as a person understands and accepts the reality of this cycle. Like Wilson's solutions, Loehr's approach can bring about significant change quickly and with minimal intervention.

For these solutions to help you change your own narrative, you must first look introspectively at the stories you tell yourself. Why are you burned out? Why do your students have behavioral issues? Why aren't your students successful? Why do the teachers, staff, and administrators at your school get under your skin? Why does your community see your school as a failure? When you can uncover specific causes of your own negative stories, it is easier to begin the editing process to change those stories.

For example, if student success in your class is a problem, stop blaming the external factors that are out of your control, and try new methods of teaching—such as pairing concepts with stories. If you feel that you are stuck in a rut and always teaching the same thing the same way, becoming a storyteller can get you excited about teaching again. If you have students who are unsuccessful, help them become storytellers; show them how to change their own stories, while you change the stories about them that you tell to others.

If you feel powerless in implementing change at your school, accept that you can become a masterful storyteller, which in turn makes you an important leader at your school. Edit the story of your role within your school, and share the new and more positive stories with other employees. Share these stories with friends and family outside of the school, and eventually share these stories with the entire community.

When you edit these stories, you break the old cause-and-effect loop and create a new one that helps lead to success. When you edit these stories, you get yourself out of the pessimism cycle and into the optimism cycle. When your story changes, then your habits will change. When your habits change, your outlook will change. When your outlook changes, you will see greater success—and you will be much happier in your role. Being happier is a key point in both the cause-and-effect loop and the optimism cycle, and it leads to even more success.

It is imperative that educators use storytelling to improve their teaching and their schools. It is imperative that educators reflect upon current narratives, understand how the existing stories came about, and work to rewrite and improve these stories. It is imperative that educators work to edit their own stories in order to be happier in their careers and create a healthier educational environment for everyone. When the stories change, students will benefit and be more successful. And that is what education is all about.

KEY POINTS FROM CHAPTER 11

Chapter 11 summarizes nine important steps covered in this book:

- Step 1: Recognize the power of story.
- Step 2: Trust that you can become a great storyteller.
- Step 3: Tell the right stories.
- Step 4: Tell the right stories at the right time.
- Step 5: Learn to tell stories in a variety of modalities.
- Step 6: Give students a chance to tell their own stories.
- Step 7: Change the stories you tell about your students.
- Step 8: Change the stories you tell about your school.
- Step 9: Change the stories you tell about yourself.

Step 9 may be the most difficult step, because it requires you to address the roadblocks preventing you from reaching your goals, and because it requires you to acknowledge your own faults, flaws, and limitations.

If you can change your own stories, you will find that you will be more effective in your job and happier in your situation.

Appendix

Examples of Stories Written by Students

The idea of having students tell their own stories was suggested several times in this book. There are many benefits to encouraging students to tell their own stories. When students relate something from their own lives to the concepts you are teaching, your students are demonstrating critical thinking skills. When your students practice writing their own stories, they are improving their storytelling skills—an extremely useful tool for their careers and their lives.

There is another important benefit: Telling personal stories is an important part of healing. Many of your students may have been through unimaginable challenges and trauma. When students tell their stories, it helps them cope and gets them back on track. Telling their stories is therapeutic and helps them reconnect with family, friends, and society. Telling their stories helps them become stronger. Sometimes their stories will simply break your heart, but they can make you stronger as well.

When your students share their personal stories with you, you get to know them as people. You begin to understand them as individuals and have a better sense of how you can connect with them and help them learn. When you hear your students' stories, you can become a more effective teacher. When you know the negative stories they tell about themselves, you can help them change those stories into positive ones.

What follows is a collection of stories written by students. These stories are from students in a college biology class and were written as part of an extra-credit assignment to relate personal experiences to something they learned in a biology class. The students posted their stories on a website so they could be shared with other students. Regardless of the subject area or the age group, reading these stories will give you some idea of what your students are capable of and how meaningful these assignments can be.

The authors of the stories that follow are anonymous. Some of these stories have been shortened a bit in order to leave out some of the medical and/or biology-related jargon and just focus on the personal story. But all of these stories are authentic and in the students' own words.

IT WAS JUST A LITTLE BRAIN SURGERY

It was late October 1999. The weather was just starting to get a bit chilly. My friend Sarah and I were driving back from her sister's apartment in Oro Valley. We were about to make a left-hand turn to take the backroads home. I remember accelerating. Then the next thing I remember is having my foot jammed on the gas and the car being embedded in a mound of dirt in a construction site that just moments before had been in front of us. I was a bit confused and had no recollection of what just happened.

After making sure Sarah was okay, I asked her what had happened. She told me I had gotten a dazed look on my face and accelerated but never turned the steering wheel to make my turn. We called her father so he could use his truck and a tow strap to pull my car out of the dirt. Sarah hardly said a word to me and kept looking at me strangely. I was too embarrassed and worried about potential damage to my car to think about what her behavior meant or what had really happened. I just wanted to get home.

The next day I knew I had to see a doctor. I had somehow lost consciousness long enough to wreck my car. Thankfully there was no real damage to the car but I had no idea what these events could mean. Since I didn't have a regular doctor, I began calling various physicians, asking if they accepted my insurance and if they were taking new patients. After several calls, I finally found a doctor, and made an appointment for the next day.

Later that night Sarah came over. After asking me about the car and making small talk, she told me she needed to tell me something. She said after I wrecked the car, I had said some "weird" things. I had no idea what she was talking about. I still couldn't remember anything about the accident. She finally told me that right after we wrecked, I had told her that "the bad man" made me do it. At first I laughed. I thought she was kidding. Who would say something so ridiculous?

I quickly realized she was serious. That was why she had been acting so strange around me after the accident. Now I was not only more embarrassed but I was growing very worried. I didn't like not remembering things I had done or said.

The next day was my doctor's appointment. After again detailing everything that happened, my doctor told me she would have to do some tests but that she thought she knew what was going on. She told me there was a good chance that I had suffered a partial complex seizure and that I was more than likely epileptic. She made an appointment for an EEG (electroencephalogram) for the following week. She explained this would confirm if I had had a seizure or not. She prescribed me a medication called Dilantin and ordered some blood samples. She told me to keep her informed if I had any more episodes that could be seizures.

During the next month, everything deteriorated quickly. The EEG came back positive for seizures. I began having multiple seizures daily. I went back to the doctor several times a week to have my blood drawn. Since the number of seizures per day was increasing rapidly, so was the amount of medication prescribed to me. The Dilantin made me so tired and lethargic—all I wanted to do was sleep. I quickly gained 20 pounds over the next month. It was depressing to think that I was going to have to deal with this for the rest of my life.

My doctor had assured me that we would eventually find the right amount of medication and get some control over the seizures, but I was losing hope fast. Things seemed to only be getting worse, with no hope of slowing down. I couldn't drive and had to be dropped off everywhere. I was a full-time student but barely had the energy for school anymore. Each day was filled with embarrassing episodes of me having a seizure, making odd statements, and looking dazed. It was hard to even go out in public.

My doctor had told me during the first week of treatment that I would need an MRI scan just to make sure there was nothing else causing the seizures. However, there was currently a waiting list. By mid-December, my doctor called. She was concerned that my seizures were happening so frequently despite the high dose of medication I was on. She had a colleague who owed her a favor at a local hospital, and he agreed to get me in for an MRI sooner than expected. My appointment was for the last week in December. I just saw it as another formality. At least it was during winter break at school.

The house phone rang on New Year's Eve at about 4:30 p.m. I was surprised that my doctor was calling me. She stated the MRI had shown an abnormal mass on the left temporal lobe of my brain. She said a neurosurgeon would call me the next day. I am not sure what I had expected her to tell me, but it definitely wasn't this. I was in shock. I dropped the phone, started crying, and went for a walk to compose myself. I was 19 years old and had a brain tumor.

By the time I had gotten back from my walk, the shock had worn off. So they wanted to cut into my brain? That's OK, I would deal with it, just like I had dealt with everything that had come my way before now. When I got to the house, my mother was outside talking with Sarah's mother, who was also our next-door neighbor. Apparently she had picked up the phone after I dropped it, and my doctor had filled her in.

To her credit, I get much of my survivor attitude from my mother. She had lost my father to brain injuries he suffered in a motorcycle accident while working undercover with the Sheriff's Department when I was only five years old. She approached this situation much as she had approached life in general since that day. She told me we would take it one day at a time and figure it out.

The neurosurgeon called me on New Year's Day. He was very blunt and direct. He told me he was one of the best in his field. He said he had a cancellation on January 4 and offered to give me the appointment, but I had to let him know right then. I asked him if there was a chance the seizures would go away once the brain tumor was removed. He told me there was a chance. He advised me he couldn't be sure whether I would need chemotherapy or radiation until after the tumor was removed and they were able to confirm whether it was cancerous or not.

Even though I had no time to research the neurosurgeon, his training, or his past surgeries, I decided he had to be extremely confident for a reason and told him to "count me in." In a span of five days I went from believing I was epileptic to finding out I had a brain tumor to having a craniotomy.

I filled those few days before surgery convincing myself that I would be seizure-free after the craniotomy. The possibility excited me and kept me from being scared, that is, until I was signing the release paperwork the day before surgery and promising my family wouldn't sue the hospital should I die on the operating table. Talk about a lot for a 19-year-old to handle!

My brain surgery took about six and a half hours. The tumor removed was one inch by three quarters of an inch in size. I looked ridiculous with half of my hair shaved off and 52 staples in my head. I had a constant headache for the first three months after surgery. But I was happy. My tumor was benign, or noncancerous. The neurosurgeon didn't feel I would benefit from chemotherapy or radiation at this time. I returned to school as soon as winter break was over, against doctor's orders, since I was tired of lying around at home.

I was told to stay on my antiseizure medication for two months after surgery. At that time, another EEG was performed, and it was determined that my last seizure had been the day prior to surgery. I was given the option to get off Dilantin. However, I was told that if I had another seizure, it would be three months before I could drive again. I chose to stop taking the medicine as soon as they offered me the chance.

I am proud to say I have remained seizure-free ever since. I get a new MRI scan every three years to make sure the tumor hasn't returned. I was told the type of tumor I had, a pilocytic astrocytoma, is known to come back, and each time it does, it's usually more invasive. I am not too worried about this possibility. I refuse to ever live my life in fear or dwelling on "what if."

I find two things troubling about my story. The first is that I had complained of chronic headaches ever since I was a little kid. When I was very young, they told me it was sinus pressure. As I became a teenager, they told me I suffered from migraines. None of my doctors ever ordered an MRI to make sure it wasn't something else. They could have prevented so much drama in my life by doing so.

The most troubling part of this story for me is that despite all I have overcome, despite how lucky I was, I am still dealing with the repercussions of having a brain tumor. The military refuses to enlist me due to a history of seizures. I have been discriminated against in various career fields as well. My last seizure, as well as my brain surgery, occurred almost 11 years ago. Yet I am still punished for something beyond my control. But I know what I was put here on Earth to do, and *nothing*, not even a little brain surgery, will hold me back.

THE WEEK I ALMOST LOST MY SON

Many first-time parents are the types that worry and over-worry about every little nuance of their angels. Any wrong cough or sniffle has them calling their pediatrician at 1 a.m. and freaking out, much to the doctor's chagrin. This is a story about me, the least overprotective mother that ever lived, and my son, Robert.

Robert was born April 1990. He was a happy, healthy baby, with no problems to speak of. His nickname was Butterman, because at three months he was almost 16 pounds. Robert was my little butterball. One morning, when he was around four months or so, he was very irritable, not wanting to eat or drink, pulling his legs into his chest, screaming, and his stomach seemed bloated.

Not really sure what was going on, I figured he was gassy and that once he relieved himself, he would begin to feel better. Well, that didn't happen. He soon had a fever to go with the discomfort, and he was vomiting a little. I called the pediatrician, and since it was after hours, he suggested I take him to the emergency room. Off we went to the hospital.

When he observed my son in the ER, the doctor thought that he might just be a little colicky with a bit of a bug bothering him. He told me, "Don't worry," and sent me on my way. He did, however, mention that I should return immediately if Robert's condition became worse or if he had bloody stools. Again, I'm not worrying too much, as the doctor has given me reassurance that Robert was OK. Nine hours later, with still not much fluid intake and after a long—very long—night, Robert had the feared bloody stool, the consistency of jelly. This is not good! And we immediately raced back to the ER. It turned out Robert was suffering from an intussusception.

An intussusception occurs when one portion of the bowel slides into the next, much like the pieces of a telescope. When this occurs, it can create a blockage in the bowel, with the walls of the intestines pressing against one another. This, in turn leads to swelling, inflammation, and decreased blood flow to the part of the intestines involved. As I was told in layman's terms, basically, if you were to take your tube sock off, it generally folds over on itself as you remove it, and this is what happened to Robert.

Treatment involved a barium enema. Once the fluid mixture is passed through the intestine, the intestine will unfold itself and fix the problem. Robert had this treatment done and stayed in the hospital for a day or two until he was eating and having normal bowel movements. Intussusception occurs most often in babies between five and 10 months of age (80% of cases occur before a child is 24 months old), affects between one and four infants out of 1,000, and is more common in boys than in girls.

Unfortunately, the story does not end there. Here is where the Mama Bear (me) had to come out. And boy, did it come out! After about four days at home, Robert still was not behaving quite right. He really wasn't interested in food and every time he took a full bottle, he would vomit. Over the next three days, we were in and out of the emergency room, and I was told that I was being an overprotective mother. But I knew there was something wrong with my child.

Finally, I told the hospital that unless they kept him for observation for a day or two, I would sue the hospital and every single person who had contact with us. Only then did they realize that he was dehydrated, and they hooked him up to a fluid IV—and he immediately began projectile vomiting. For those not familiar with projectile vomit, it literally flies across the room and hits the walls. I'd already been dealing with that for three days, so it was nothing new to me. But what came out of his mouth now made the hospital realize something was seriously wrong with him. He was vomiting stools.

For 10 days, Robert was in the hospital. For four of them, doctors were telling me they did not know what was wrong with Robert, but they tried to prepare me in case he passed away. I lived at the hospital with him. On the fifth day, his surgeon said he wanted to go into Robert's abdomen for exploratory surgery to see if he could find anything wrong. Luckily, he did.

The intussusception had caused about three inches of Robert's intestine to die. When they first did the barium enema, the problem was corrected, but the tissue perforated and, as it tried to heal, it adhered to his stomach lining. So basically, his intestinal track was blocked, and it ended at the stomach adhesions. Once they removed the dead tissue and reconnected good tissue, Robert made a swift recovery.

Robert's complications were new to nearly everyone in the medical profession, which was why no one recognized the symptoms. Our doctors had consulted with others throughout the country, and until the surgery, no one could offer any solutions. Robert did become famous in some medical circles, as his case was written up in the New England Journal of Medicine. Hopefully, no other family has had to suffer the way we did.

Today, Robert is a healthy 22-year-old man. He's never had a relapse, although relapses are common with those who have had an intussusception. For all you Mama Bears out there, don't let the medical profession bully you into thinking you don't know what is best for your kids. Sometimes you have to be the one who is in the doctors' faces, fighting for your kids.

LIVING WITH A RARE CONDITION

When my mother was 18, she was pregnant with her first child. As if it wasn't hard enough being a teenage mom, my mother's first child was diagnosed with a very rare condition, and that child was me. My name is Carol, and I am living with hereditary angioedema.

Hereditary angioedema (HAE) is a rare disease of the immune system, affecting an estimated one in 10,000 people. HAE causes attacks of spontaneous swelling that are often painful and severe. The most common locations of HAE attacks are the hands, feet, face, genitals, abdomen, and throat. I experience HAE attacks at least once a week, or if I'm lucky, once every two weeks.

HAE attacks last between two and five days. HAE attacks are very unpredictable and can happen anywhere at any time. When it is my face, genitals, hands, or feet, it is extremely uncomfortable, disfiguring, and embarrassing. When it is my abdomen, it is severely painful and causes nonstop vomiting, and I always have to be hospitalized for abdominal attacks. Last but not least, when it is my throat, it is the most dangerous because it can block my breathing. It is an extremely scary and uncomfortable feeling, and I also have to be hospitalized for this attack.

When I was two years old, it was late at night and my mom woke up to me crying. She turned the lights on and found that my face was severely swollen. Doctors could not figure out what was wrong with me until I turned seven years old and was diagnosed with HAE. I am now 19 years old, and living with this condition has been a constant challenge. When I was 17 years old, my throat got swollen, and I completely stopped breathing and had to be intubated. It was one of the worst feelings and worst experiences ever in my life. Thankfully I survived and got through it.

After all these years you learn to deal with it and accept that you will live with this for the rest of your life. I might as well make the best of it! I tend to handle my attacks very well and try not to make a big deal out of them. I try to act as if I'm okay, but the truth is that every time I have an attack, I feel miserable, not just physically but emotionally as well. It is a very sad and bitter feeling, as there are many things I miss out on and cannot do because of this condition.

I am basically living my life inside a bubble, and I try my best not to have bitter feelings. But sometimes I think to myself, "Why me?" I know there are people out there experiencing much worse things than I am, and for that reason I am not a bitter person, and I am still grateful for the life that I have. Although I have had to live most of my life in a bubble, I have still been able to accomplish many things such as graduating high school with my class, starting my first year of college, moving out of my home, and living on my own in a new city.

However, there is one medication out there that could help prevent all of my attacks and possibly allow me to live a normal, pain-free life. This medication is an injection that I would need three times a week. I have tried and tried to get this medication, but my insurance won't cover it and I simply cannot afford it. I have not given up on getting this medication, and I have started a new program that will hopefully help me get this medication. It has been over a year now of fighting for this treatment that I still do not have, but I will keep on fighting until I am finally able to receive it.

I hope by sharing my story people will become more aware of this condition and also be thankful and grateful for the life that they have, because there are people out there who could be experiencing much worse situations.

LIVING WITH AIDS

This is the story of Hanna, my very best friend, and how she lived with AIDS. She lived every day to the fullest, and so many people looked up to her. It was hard to see her go, but when she did, she was ready, because she felt she had fulfilled her purpose.

Hanna was born HIV-positive. Her biological mother was HIV-positive and was a heavy drug user. Hanna spent a month in the hospital when she was born due to a cocaine addiction she acquired during her mother's pregnancy. Hanna was left abandoned in an apartment by her mother when Hanna was only two years old, and she went through many abusive foster homes. At the age of six, she was diagnosed with AIDS. She was treated cruelly in the foster homes where she lived.

Back then not much was known about AIDS, so even at the hospital, the doctors always wore gloves and face masks around her. One foster family actually put Hanna outside with the dogs because they didn't want her around them or the other children! She was finally adopted at the age of nine into an awesome home with a great mother figure. When she was adopted, the doctors told her new mom that Hanna would not live to the age of twelve.

She definitely showed them. She was one of the longest-living kids born with HIV.

The earlier years of Hanna's life were the hardest because people didn't really know the facts about the virus. When she enrolled in a school, parents would pull their kids out of her classes, or she would be required by school officials to have an aide with her at all times. She was completely isolated and stereotyped as the "contagious girl."

Hanna finally got fed up with the stories and lies that are constantly told about AIDS and HIV and ways of contracting the virus. In high school she started her life's work to educate people. She spoke at high schools, colleges, and World AIDS Day events, and she did a lot of work with the Southern Arizona AIDS Foundation. I went with her to several of her speeches, and it was always interesting to see the surprised faces of her audience because she did not look sickly. In fact, she looked like a really vibrant young woman.

Her audience always had so many misconceptions at every speech she gave. Most of the audience expected a sickly person who contracted HIV through sex. When she stood in front of groups of people and told them it's not always transmitted through sex and how long she has been living with AIDS and how there is no cure but she was taking a cocktail of 30 pills a day, chins would drop to the floor.

Unfortunately, even though the cocktail of drugs did help to prolong her life, they also made her really sick. She would have to go on and off the drugs due to their being so toxic to her body. It was really hard for Hanna to keep down any sort of food, and what with taking the cocktail of pills on top of that, she could basically forget about eating. Her diet consisted mainly of Sustacal because even the Marinol pills that she was given did not help her keep food down. She began losing weight and had a chronic cough that would rack her body.

She ended up having to have a port put into her chest that looked a lot like a pacemaker but was instead used for IV connections, because her veins just shut down. She would come over and bring her IV bags with her, and we would sit in my room and do our nails, watch movies, and have girl talk while her IV bag, hanging off my bunk bed, was connected to her chest. I don't know how she did it, but she even made carrying around an oxygen tank look good. She was very outgoing and confident in herself, and she was able to live a life that she was proud of.

I just want people to know that a person with HIV and AIDS could be a neighbor or a best friend. People with AIDS are not always emaciated or sickly looking with lesions. There are so many other misconceptions that are out there. AIDS is not always contracted through sex. People with AIDS are no different from anyone else, and instead of condemning them for having AIDS, it's important to remember that they are fighting a battle within their bodies every day to live. Support, friendship, and acceptance are really important, and society needs to understand this—and get the facts straight!

A REFLECTION ON MY LIFE SO FAR

My Early Years: I was born in Hyderabad, India, on September 27, 1992. After I was born, my biological parents left me in the hospital because I was born without fully developed arms or legs—just short stumps where my arms and legs should have been. After my parents left the hospital without me, I was sent to an orphanage.

In India, most people are poor, and so when someone is disabled, the family will often send the person out to beg on the streets. The family may also just neglect or reject disabled family members, and so such persons are forced to live on the streets and beg for the rest of their lives. My biological parents spared me the life of begging, and they instead gave me the present of living, in the form of adoption. At the age of five, I was adopted and came to the United States of America!

Dog Years: A friend of mine had a dog who had a litter of puppies. Every week after the puppies were born, my adoptive father and I would go over and see the puppies. One week I got on the floor and was playing with them when I noticed that one of the puppies wasn't playing with the others. Behind the other young dogs, there was one puppy all by himself. I went over and picked up the puppy and sat on a chair. The puppy seemed so happy sitting on my lap, and as I was petting the puppy, the other dogs were attacking my shorts. I ended up getting that puppy, and I named him Ravi. In Hindi, *Ravi* means "the sun," and at the age of eight, I had my first dog.

A year later Ravi and I began to go through Top Dog, which is an organization that helps people with physical disabilities train their own service dogs. I was the youngest person to go through Top Dog. In 2004, Ravi and I were certified as Top Dog Team 78. Before I retired Ravi at the age of 10, I started training my second service dog, Ashka. Ashka and I were certified as Top Dog Team 108 in the summer of 2011. Sadly, just one year later, Ravi died of valley fever.

Blessing in Disguise: When I was in the second grade, I started dealing with bone overgrowth. Bone overgrowth is a condition when the bone grows faster than the skin can keep up. So in other words, the bone will go through the skin. When this happens it is very painful. Since my arms and legs are so short, the likelihood of bone overgrowth happening on all of my limbs is high.

When bone overgrowth happens, the only way of dealing with it is to have surgery. The surgery consists of shaving back the bone and putting either a hip graft or Teflon at the end of the limb. I have had several surgeries on my short limbs, including five surgeries on my right arm, three on my left arm, one on my right leg, and one on my left leg. After each surgery it would take me six weeks to recover. I have had 17 surgeries, with 10 of them being bone overgrowth surgeries. But each one of the surgeries was a blessing in disguise—each one of them helped make me a stronger person.

LIVING WITH EPILEPSY

A seizure is a sudden surge of electrical activity in the brain that usually affects how a person feels or acts for a short time. Having seizures is not a disease by itself; rather, seizures are a symptom of many different disorders that can affect the brain. Some seizures can hardly be noticed, while others are totally disabling.

The seizures in epilepsy may be related to a brain injury or a family tendency, but often the cause is completely unknown. The word *epilepsy* does not indicate anything about the cause or severity of the person's seizures.

At the age of five, I was diagnosed with grand mal seizures. A grand mal seizure is caused by abnormal electrical activity throughout the brain. In some cases, this type of seizure is triggered by other health problems, such as extremely low blood sugar or a stroke. Most of the time, however, a grand mal seizure is caused by epilepsy. Many people who have a grand mal seizure will never have another one. However, some people need daily anti-seizure medications to control grand mal seizures.

In my case I was prescribed a daily medicine because I had been diagnosed with epilepsy. Sometimes seizures can be set off by the smallest inconsistency with your schedule, such as not enough sleep, too much stress, or a bad diet. My seizures always happened when I didn't get enough sleep or I felt stressed. On almost every vacation I went on when I was younger, I had a seizure.

I remember being so excited to go to Disneyland one year that I could not sleep the night before. I was up in the morning getting ready, and all of a sudden I woke up with my parents standing around me yelling my name. I was not aware of what had just happened or why I was on the ground. I stood up and instantly felt sick.

In some cases people can have a seizure and be fine the rest of the day. In my case, if I have a seizure, seizures will continue to happen throughout the day until I raise the dose of my medicine. Instead of taking me to Disneyland, my parents took me to the hospital so they could give me an IV with the medicine in it. Afterward, I was fine but had to continue to take higher doses of my medicine.

One of the medications I was prescribed was Depakote. Depakote (divalproex sodium) affects chemicals in the body that may be involved in causing seizures. Depakote is used to treat various types of seizure disorders. It is sometimes used together with other seizure medications. As with any medication, there are always side effects. With strong medicines like Depakote, you can expect stronger side effects, including hair loss, memory loss, and emotional problems.

I was in fourth grade when I started taking Depakote on a daily basis. After I started taking Depakote, my teachers noticed my grades starting to drop. I went to my neurologist, and my mom told him about what my teachers had said to her, and the doctor made me take a written test. I wasn't sure what the test was for at the time, but now I know the test was to measure how well my memory was working. After taking the test, I was diagnosed with short-term memory loss caused by the Depakote.

We decided to try other medications instead of Depakote to see if something else would help the seizures and not affect my memory, but the other medications did not work, so I was stuck with Depakote. Today I cannot recall many of the family vacations we took when I was younger, and I can only reminisce with the pictures that were taken. It's sad sometimes when my sister will ramble on about how much fun we had on a certain vacation that I can't remember, but I am sure I had just as much fun.

I was on Depakote up until about a year ago. I had experienced minimal seizures while on Depakote. The only reason I had any seizures was that I was not good about taking my medicine when I was a teenager, so the levels of the drug in my body were not consistent. I had not had any seizures for a while and I had felt I had grown out of having seizures, so I took myself off the medication.

I recently told my neurologist that I had not been taking my medicine for about a year. We decided we would do an EEG scan to see if there was any abnormal activity in my brain. We got the results back and nothing was found on the EEG. He said that can happen sometimes, so to be sure I would have to do three more scans, and have all of them come back normal, to be completely sure. I have my second scan soon and I am crossing my fingers that it turns out normal! But even if the scan isn't normal, I will continue to do all the things any normal person would do!

KABUKI SYNDROME

My daughter Caroline was born with a rare genetic condition called Kabuki Syndrome. Caroline was a planned baby, and I was very careful about getting appropriate exercise, eating a balanced diet, and not taking medications. The pregnancy overall was relatively normal, other than really bad "afternoon sickness" as opposed to "morning sickness." By the time she was delivered, I had gained a total of 20 pounds and was in good health. Her delivery, however, was anything but normal.

When Caroline was born, the umbilical cord was wrapped around her neck four times. She was not breathing and was a "blue baby." The medical staff was finally able to get her heart going again. Caroline's first two Apgar scores (the tests taken to assess the health of a newborn), were only a "4," whereas healthy babies should be a "7" or higher. We also noticed multiple congenital anomalies, and the doctors ran tests to see if she had Down Syndrome. But it wasn't Down Syndrome. My husband and I left the hospital not knowing what was wrong with our daughter.

Caroline soon began having ear infections, and by the time she was four years old she had six different sets of tubes in her ears (she kept developing allergies to them) and had her adenoids removed twice. By the age of five, she was lucky if she was off antibiotics for more than two weeks at a time. She developed allergies to a lot of the antibiotics and now has a limited variety available to her.

On the scale of developmental milestones, she was always on the low side of normal but not enough to cause serious concern. We took her for genetics counseling as a baby, but no one could identify what syndrome she fit into. It wasn't until she was 11 years old that she was diagnosed with Kabuki Syndrome, which very few people even knew about, and at that time the cause was unknown. Caroline is one of the older children diagnosed with this syndrome.

Kabuki Syndrome, previously known as Kabuki Makeup Syndrome or Niikawa-Kuroki Syndrome, is a very rare syndrome affecting roughly one in every 32,000 births. It has a genetic origin with multiple congenital disorders typically affecting intellectual disabilities and some physical abilities as well. It wasn't identified and classified until 1981, by two Japanese groups led by the scientists Niikawa and Kuroki (hence the name). The term *Kabuki Syndrome* is used because of the resemblance to faces with makeup applied in a Japanese traditional theatrical dance-drama form of entertainment called Kabuki.

Individual phenotypes can vary from case to case, but the overriding features appear to be hypotonia (poor muscle tone), a high incidence of cleft palate (Caroline did not have this), and feeding difficulties regardless of having cleft palate. Other musculoskeletal features may include brachydactyly (short fingers), brachymesophalangy (abnormally short bones), and clinodactyly (turning in of the fifth finger), as well as spinal anomalies, including scoliosis (bending of the spine).

Babies with Kabuki Syndrome often grow reasonably well inside the womb but grow very slowly after birth. Facial features typically include long eyelids (palpebral fissures) with the turning-out of the outer third of the lower eyelid, arched eyebrows with a thin outer half, prominent eyelashes, prominent and/or misshapen ears, and a flattened nasal tip. There are many more anomalies which are too numerous to list here, and this is why Kabuki Syndrome was originally so difficult to categorize into one syndrome.

In 2010, University of Washington researchers announced the discovery of the MLL2 gene mutations that are responsible for approximately 75% of individuals with Kabuki Syndrome. The deletion of a single nucleotide leads to a change in the protein that is produced. It is unknown at this point how the changes to the gene change the function of protein or why it causes the features of Kabuki syndrome. It is also unknown if different changes within the gene can lead to more or less severe clinical features. Most individuals with Kabuki will have normal chromosomal study test results, and this was true of my daughter too.

Caroline was homeschooled for most of the years she was in school. I wanted to make sure that she could develop as fully as possible. Up until she was 11, we didn't know what was happening with her genetically and what health or educational issues she would have. She was, and still is, very bright with above-average memorization, reading, and algebra skills. She is highly disciplined, very intuitive, and lots of fun to be with.

Her weaknesses are in sentence and paragraph structuring as well as spelling. Caroline graduated with honors from an accredited online high school in all mainstream classes. At this point in her life (she's now a young adult), she is still not able to cross the streets safely, and she lacks some of the social skills and day-to-day living skills that most people pick up naturally. But she is currently in vocational rehabilitation to develop job skills and is taking online college classes this fall. I couldn't be more proud of my beautiful daughter!

MAJOR DEPRESSIVE DISORDER

In 2000, Randy went to his primary care doctor to talk to him about some new, unusual feelings he was experiencing. In the preceding months, he had noticed that he was feeling what to him felt like an unnatural amount of anxiety. He was often finding himself curled up in the corner of his room, distraught from waves of terrible feelings. He also noticed he was easily agitated, had horrible headaches, and his body hurt so bad that he didn't want to move.

Randy's doctor referred him to a psychiatrist who diagnosed Randy with major depressive disorder. The psychiatrist and the team of doctors working with him quickly started Randy on a mix of medications to help combat his symptoms. They thought they could get him to the point where he would feel comfortable enough in his own skin again, and he could continue living his life the way he was before all this happened.

Randy is a divorced single father of three boys and one girl. Raising his children on his own had never posed a problem for him. Money was tight, but he always made it work. He was a building inspector, and he parented his children with an authoritative parenting style. His children, from youngest to oldest, were 10, 12, 16, and 18; the youngest was his only daughter.

In 2000, it seemed like many things happened for Randy all at once. He was diagnosed with hepatitis C, a bowel disorder, and degenerative joint disease. He made the choice to quit smoking cigarettes (which he had been doing since he was a young boy), and this further increased his anxiety. But he knew that for his health, he had to give up the cigarettes.

Then his youngest son started smoking marijuana and taking Randy's truck out for joyrides, his middle son started drinking heavily, and his oldest was experimenting with a lot of hard drugs. Randy soon discovered that the other parents from the children's school were starting to judge him. One parent was so convinced she could do better that she tried to get legal custody of his youngest son. She changed her mind after a few months, when the boy stole her car.

On top of all of that, there were some very bad problems at work, with big-name companies trying to bribe him to pass their inspections. He had to take medical leave for surgery for his bowels, but the surgery wasn't done right, and the result was that he couldn't even sit on his bottom, making him even more embarrassed and uncomfortable. Soon his medical leave ran out and he was let go from his job. He decided to try early retirement, but there was no way the money would last until his youngest could even finish high school.

With all this happening, the medication for his depression was just not helping, and he often found himself unable to even get out of bed most mornings. His medical insurance from work ran out, but he was lucky that as a veteran, he could be seen by the VA. The new psychiatrist at the VA decided to try a new mix of medication and has been trying different mixtures ever since. At Randy's last appointment, the doctor said he was not going to give up on him and that he is confident he can find the right mix of medication for Randy.

When I ask my dad if he feels better, he states that he only feels like 25% of his "normal" self. He knows the medication helps because he doesn't find himself in the corner anymore, but it is still hard to get him out of the house. My dad thinks he can't give up hope for being fully better, but he only plans to take it one day at a time. One of the emotions he misses most about himself is the feeling of being comfortable in his own skin, especially when he is in a crowd.

My dad looks back over the last eleven years and understands that the best plausible explanation for his major depressive disorder is that everything happened in such a short period of time. I think he knows that he could have handled each of these events individually, but when all these events happened in the same year, it was just too much.

Some of the stressors have improved. My dad no longer has any connection to the people he once worked with, he finally got the correct surgery for his bowels, and he has learned to live with and cope with his hepatitis C and degenerative joint disease. He had a minor heart attack a few years ago, and that served as a reminder to manage his stress and health to the best of his ability.

Randy's oldest son grew out of what he was doing, is finishing college, and is happily married. His two youngest sons still give him a hard time and are still dealing with behavior issues, but two years ago Randy made a breakthrough in accepting that it is not entirely his fault. Ironically, it was his daughter (me!) who decided to pursue a degree in psychology and was the first-ever college graduate in the family.

My dad never even told me about some of his diagnoses until my junior year, when I was in my second abnormal psychology class. I graduated in 2011 and will never stop telling him to try things other than just medications for his major depressive disorder. Even though I didn't put it together that my dad had these diagnoses and problems, it is all so clear to me now when I look back on it. Living through it with him gave me such a different perspective. I knew there was something really wrong, but I was so young when it happened, I guess I just didn't catch on.

When the problems began, I always did my best to not make my dad sad, to make it easier around the house for him, and to just try and fade into the background so I wasn't an added stressor. I knew that no matter what, he would always love me, and the love was still there, but it was just him who felt so far away. I think after he opened up to me about his disorder, I was able to feel more of that connection and at least understand what was happening, but it still doesn't feel the same. I think we both know it; the whole family knows it.

All the pieces needed for a close-knit family are still there, but there is just something keeping all of us from coming together like the way things had been before. I hope we are able to get him back fully, but I wonder, because of how long it has been, if we will even notice when we get him back. I think that is one of my bigger fears. Another big fear is that he will never feel better, and that we will always remember that there was a "better time" and just accept what we have now.

Even with all the improvements, my dad's self-esteem is still very low, and there are times when I notice he has not showered in almost a week. He states that there is no reason to shower when he is not planning on doing anything. I get so frustrated, because I know he is not a dumb person, but I don't understand why he can't see what he is doing to himself. Lately my brothers and I have teamed up to get on him about him showering and about his self-esteem. I think that over the last few months, he has been working on his hygiene more; but when I think about it, I just hear his words in my head: "one day at a time." So that is what this family does now: living one day at a time.

I WISH I COULD BE EINSTEIN

Ever since I was a child, I always felt like I was extremely intelligent. In elementary school, I picked up reading faster than the other children. It wasn't long before I was reading 900-page novels at a college level—while I was still in second grade. I also picked up mathematics faster than the other children. It just seemed that I had a knack for school.

However, these gifts weren't given without some drawbacks. Much of the time, I had an extreme lack of focus or motivation. Even with the ability to easily do the work or participate fully in class, I chose not to. I didn't feel as if I was lazy; I just didn't know how to succeed. Later I was diagnosed with ADHD (attention-deficit hyperactivity disorder). I attribute my lack of focus, lack of motivation, and poor organizational skills to this disease of my brain.

When I was first prescribed Ritalin, it gave me a focus that I never had before. I was able to complete my work on time and consistently earn A grades. It didn't give me any harsh side effects, but after a while it just stopped working. Even when it did work, it almost felt like my mom was nagging me to do my homework. The motivation didn't come from within, so I decided I needed a change. My doctor was going to give me a higher dosage of Ritalin, but instead I opted to switch to Adderall.

When I started taking Adderall, it was like a miracle drug for me. I felt as if there was a laser beam from God shining on my homework, pushing me to do my best. I excelled, doing much better than when I was on Ritalin. The only downfall to this medication was that I felt that it took away all my creativity. Normally when I write essays, I am a great writer, and the words just seem to flow onto the paper. However, with Adderall, sometimes I feel as if I'm wearing blinders and not able to think properly and fully. Essentially, this drug was not allowing me to see outside the box, as if it gave me tunnel vision. No longer was I writing masterpieces but merely boring papers that had no grammatical errors at all.

Even my character and personality were affected by Adderall. My girlfriend has grown to love me as the wild, rambunctious person that I am without ADHD medications. I used to be wild and say and do off-the-wall, random things. She was used to that, and she loved to be around me when I was like that. However on Adderall, my girlfriend describes me as dull and boring. She often tells me she misses the crazy, funny person that I am when off the drugs, and she can't stand the boring person I've become on these medications.

Due to these repercussions of the medications, I have since decided to only take them sparingly. I know I can excel in school without them, but sometimes I feel like I need to take my medication or else I will not do well. What I hope you get from this excerpt of my life is to be the person who you want to be. I started taking this drug in hopes that it would make me a genius, forgetting I was already smart to begin with. I can succeed in school and life without this drug that turns me into a zombie. As long as you are happy with who you are, that is all that matters.

TWO HEARTS MENDED FOR LIFE

This story is about my husband John and me—my name is Pat—when we were 35 and 34 years old, respectively. Our story starts in 1997. We were living in a small town in New Mexico when, one day, I went to the doctor with what I thought was a chest cold. After weeks of tests and medicines, I was finally diagnosed with cardiomyopathy, which I was told was "heart muscle disease."

I was told to head to the hospital and check myself in. I did. The first doctor I saw told me to get my affairs in order. In fact, when he came in, I was on the phone with my mother, who lived in California at the time, and he told her to get to my side as soon as she could get here. I'll never forget his words: "Your daughter is dying." We were scared out of our minds!

Then a different doctor came in and gave us a very different prognosis. He told us that since I had just given birth three months prior, the disease was considered to be of peripartum onset and would either go away or kill me. As time passed and I was getting better, we started to let go of our fears. It seemed as though I had beaten it. Nearly two years later, we went to the doctor, and he gave us the good news: I had indeed beaten this disease! He took me off all medicines, released me from his care, and cleared me to work. We were overjoyed, and life went back to normal for my husband and me and our two-year-old son.

About two years later, I was working as a restaurant manager, and I began to notice that I was tiring more easily and getting short of breath. I immediately went into denial and ignored the symptoms. As the symptoms got worse, I finally made an appointment to see the doctor. I was terrified when I heard the diagnosis: cardiomyopathy! It was back, and this time with a vengeance. My heart went from its normal size to almost double in size.

This time the doctor told me that my disease was not going away. He said I had a very serious, life-threatening disease. He put me on a regimen of heart medicines and sent me home. Remember now, I was in a very small New Mexican town where the medical community was not nearly as progressive as it is here in Tucson. So, here I am with the news that the disease had returned, and this time it was not going away. In fact, it was going to kill me for sure.

I made a vow to myself to live as long as I could with my disease. You see, I had a son to bring up! I turned completely to my faith for strength. I knew God wouldn't bless me with a child only to take his mother away from him. With that as my arsenal, I set out to live despite this ugly disease. I took my meds, exercised daily, and began a holistic regimen of herbs that aided in heart health. I never went back to that doctor—he basically told me he couldn't help me anymore.

In 1999, I found a doctor at a heart hospital in Albuquerque who followed me and my disease, and all he ever said was, "Keep doing what you're doing." So I did. I kept up with my exercise, I took my meds and my supplements, and I started eating healthier. That worked for me for several years.

Then in March 2005, in New Mexico, we opened a restaurant and it really took off. Unfortunately, around that time I began having some really bad spells of pain that I wasn't telling anyone about. I didn't want to spoil my husband's dream of owning a restaurant. For weeks, the spells kept coming and getting worse until I finally told my husband about them. By now it was June 2005. We went to the heart doctor in Albuquerque, and he told me to see a congestive heart failure specialist because I was probably in heart failure. I went about trying to find a CHF specialist in our area.

A few days later, I found a CHF specialist who would see me. Our appointment was in July, only a couple weeks later. When John came home from the restaurant that night, I was going to tell him about the CHF specialist I made an appointment with. But when I opened my mouth to talk, all of my words slurred like I was drunk. John lifted me up, put shoes on me, told my mom he was taking me to the ER, and off we went. He slaughtered the speed limit and ran lights and got me to the ER in about 20 minutes. (It's usually a 40-minute drive!)

I have to note again that we lived in a very small town, and the hospital was not sophisticated enough to handle what I had. I stayed there for four days, and then I was driven 200+ miles by ambulance to my heart hospital in Albuquerque. I don't remember anything about that time span. Most of the stay in Albuquerque was told to me by John. When I got there, I was put in a room and hooked up to IVs.

The next morning, the doctor who was taking my regular doctor's place (he was on vacation), came in yelling for the nurses to take the saline drip off. My body was retaining fluid, because my heart was too weak to supply blood to my kidneys for them to be effective in removing water and wastes. She began to hit at the machine trying to shut it off, and eventually the IV drip was stopped. At this time, I was semiconscious. So they would be effective, my meds were administered straight into my veins by injection. My heart was so weak that all of my organs were shutting down. I was in critical condition. I was dying!

They told my husband that they could give me meds that would make my heart work better. However, the strain of the medicine would make my heart weaker, eventually killing me. He decided I should take the medicine. This is when I began to come to, and I remember what was going on. I actually began to feel better. I thought this thing was over and that I was out of the woods. But John knew better. The doctor came in, and that's when I first heard the word: "transplant"!

The doctor told me the only chance I had to survive was a heart transplant. I was terrified—again. I told the doctor that I felt better than I had in a long time. He said that the medicine that was making me feel better would eventually kill me. The meds were so dangerous to my health that as soon as I was stabilized, I was taken off them. This was only a short-term treatment. He told me I had to decide right away if I wanted to be evaluated for a heart transplant and said it was my only chance of long-term survival.

I looked around the room at my family, and it took me less than a minute to decide: "Yes, I will go for the transplant." Two days later, on July 20, 2005, Dr. Jack Copeland of UMC Tucson said his team would take me as a candidate for transplant, and later that day I was on a life flight from Albuquerque to Tucson.

While I was in Tucson being evaluated for my transplant, my husband went about moving us to Tucson. From the time I began slurring my words, I never saw my home in New Mexico again. John was very scared, as he knew little if anything about transplantation. All he knew was that he needed to get himself and our son to Tucson to be with me. So he walked away from our home. He stored what belongings he could, gave away a lot, and brought what he thought we needed to Tucson with him. So far as the restaurant goes, he walked away from it as well.

John removed our son from the only school he had known in order to bring him to Tucson. It was a lot of pressure for them to be under in such a short time. They arrived in Tucson about a week after I did. John secured a one-bedroom, one-bath apartment with the help of the hospital social worker, put our son in school (fourth grade), and set about being there for me. He visited me every day and brought our son up several times a week.

After a month of tests, I was accepted on the transplant list and listed as "A1," top of the list. I had a PIC line for constant IV meds, and an ICD, which is an implanted device that would give my heart a shock if it ever went into an abnormal rhythm. I was then released from UMC to wait for my call.

About a month later, John had taken me to UMC's transplant clinic for a routine checkup. It was in the afternoon, and our son was still in school. We waited a long time, and time was running short for us to make it to our son's school to pick him up. John decided to leave and get our son and then come back for me. About 40 minutes later, I was called into a room and saw the doctor. I kept waiting for John to walk in at any time—he should have been back and he always had questions for the doctor. But John never came in.

The doctor and I finished up, and I went out to the waiting area. To my surprise, John and our son were sitting there. I went over to John, and as soon as I reached him, I knew he didn't look right. He was sweaty and lying down as much as he could on the chair he was on. I asked him what was wrong. He said he was hot from running up four flights of stairs. I didn't buy that, because I've seen him overheated before and never had he ever sweated buckets like he was doing then. He kept telling me he just needed water and a wet towel to cool off.

I was really scared because John just didn't look like himself. I asked him if he wanted to go down to the ER to get checked, but he declined. The nurses in the clinic had gotten wind of what was going on, and they suggested he go to the ER also. With that, he agreed to go. The nurses insisted on calling transport for John to go to the ER, so we waited for the guy to bring a wheelchair to wheel him there. We were all joking and laughing at John being in a wheelchair; our son really got a kick out of it. I guess because of the transport, John was taken back right away.

After he was checked in, John was put into a room where he would be seen by the doctor. A nurse came in to take a history and to draw blood. When she came in, she did a double take because she wasn't sure who the patient was, because I looked as sick as I was. I was thin, ashen in color, and had a fanny pack around my waist with an IV drip bag filled with heart medicine to keep me alive. As she was attending to John, it came out that I was on the transplant list. I was beginning to feel better because I knew he was about to be seen by a doctor.

I grabbed a magazine and took a seat in a chair. Our son was standing next to his dad, talking to him as he lay back to get his blood drawn. He has that thing where, when blood is drawn, he has to be reclined or he could pass out. Suddenly, I heard my son yell out to his dad. I heard the nurse sternly say, "John."

I looked up to see her run her knuckles across John's chest; then I saw the worst thing that I have ever seen: I saw my husband dying. I saw his head hyperextend back—it kept going back slowly. Just then the nurse yelled at the top of her lungs, "Code Blue!" Almost instantly, the room was filled with white coats. One guy grabbed the cart and pulled out the paddles, and I yelled out, "Please save my husband!" I grabbed my son and we left the room.

A couple of hours later, I was told that my husband had a massive heart attack. "How could that be?" I asked. "He's very health-conscious and doesn't have any heart issues!" The doctor told me he survived the "widow maker," the type of heart attack that instantly kills, and had my husband been anywhere other than where he was, he'd be dead. They went in, removed the clots, and inserted stents to reopen the arteries that had closed. There was one that was 100% occluded and another that was 80% closed.

As I was already in a fog, the next question blew me away. I was asked if they could freeze my husband. "What!?" Apparently, there was this experimental treatment where, if you drop the body temperature of a person who has had a major heart attack, it minimizes possible damage to the brain. As it was explained to me, freezing halts the inflammation that kills brain cells after the brain has been deprived of oxygen for a period of time. Just then the surgeon came in and ruled out the necessity of the freezing because my husband was not "dead" long enough to do any damage. I was thankful that I didn't have to decide, because my brains were mush! Since the surgeon advised against it, I said no.

Within a couple of weeks, my husband recovered enough to be released. The cardiologist on my husband's case told us that his heart attack was stress-related. He informed us that all the stress my husband was under was just too much for him to handle. He told us that certain stresses can cause physiological changes such as increased blood pressure, elevated levels of cortisol, and changes in the way blood clots. All those changes created the perfect storm for a heart attack to occur. We've heard that stress can kill, and John was proof that it really can. Thank heavens that he was in the ER when he nearly died!

By November, John was doing much better, and I was still waiting for a new heart. Life went on, and finally on December 21, 2005, as we were eating salad at Sweet Tomatoes, my husband's phone rang. His eyes got really big, and he kept saying, "Yes! OK!" I knew it was "the call." I was to arrive at UMC by 3:00 p.m. It was already about 1:00 p.m. It was finally "my turn"!

We all arrived at UMC at 3:00 p.m. sharp, and my journey began. After all the tests and blood draws, it was nearly 7:00 p.m. when I was wheeled into surgery. I said all my "I love yous," I got my kisses and best wishes, and away I went.

Next thing I remember, I was being awakened. I felt like a brand new person. I was still hooked up to tubes galore, so I couldn't speak. My husband said my color was back, and the look on his and our son's faces were priceless. I did it! Two days later, my husband and my son brought Christmas up to my room. We opened our presents. We sang carols. Of course, I had the greatest gift ever, and it wasn't wrapped. That was my best Christmas ever.

That story took place nearly seven years ago. I am doing great, my husband is doing great, and our son is doing great. I am coming up on my seventh "transiversary." I am an organ donation advocate, and I volunteer with Donor Network of Arizona. In fact, if you go to the MVD, you may see my picture in a Donor Network of Arizona poster urging drivers to register as an organ donor on their driver's license. Please *do*!

In closing, even though this is highly personal, I must add that our son received counseling for the trauma he experienced at the age of eight. He almost lost both his parents. Counseling truly helped him. He is now a 16-year-old junior in high school, where he gets As and Bs, he is a black belt in karate, and he is a keyboardist in a band. That part of my journey ended happily, but every day is still a journey. Every day reminds us that we are living our second chance. My husband and I will always share an even deeper bond than most married couples—we are two hearts mended for life.

References

Abamu, J. (2018, September 12). DC area students tell history from their own eyes on the Hamilton stage. Retrieved from https://wamu.org/story/18/09/12/d-c-area-students-tell-history-eyes-hamilton-stage

Beyer, J. (2014, May 14). Teaching storytellers how to tell their own story. Retrieved from http://careeradvisor.blogs.american.edu/2014/05/14/students-who-are-studying-the-fields-of-public

CBS News. (2008, March 13). Dennis Quaid recounts twins' drug ordeal. *60 Minutes*. Retrieved from https://www.cbsnews.com/news/dennis-quaid-recounts-twins-drug-ordeal/3

CDC. (2014). Pandemic influenza storybook. Retrieved from https://www.cdc.gov/publications/panflu/index.html

Defining critical thinking. (2017). Retrieved from http://www.criticalthinking.org/pages/defining-critical-thinking/766

DeMers, J. (2017, July 11). Why podcasts are popular (and 4 content lessons to learn from them). *Forbes*. Retrieved from https://www.forbes.com/sites/jaysondemers/2017/07/11/why-podcasts-are-popular-and-4-content-lessons-to-learn-from-them/#4b872fa118f6

Denning, S. (2004, May). Telling tales. *Harvard Business Review*, *82*(5), 122–129.

De Salvo, L. (1999). *Writing as a way of healing: How telling our stories transforms our lives*. Boston, MA: Beacon Press.

Dickey, C. (2016, November 12). The shrink as secret agent: Jung, Hitler, and the OSS. Retrieved from https://www.thedailybeast.com/the-shrink-as-secret-agent-jung-hitler-and-the-oss

Fisher, A. (2014, February 25). Why TED Talks are better than the last speech you sat through. *Fortune*. Retrieved from http://fortune.com/2014/02/25/why-ted-talks-are-better-than-the-last-speech-you-sat-through

Fourtane, S. (2018, August 6). Thomas Midgley Jr.: The man who harmed the world the most. Retrieved from https://interestingengineering.com/thomas-midgley-jr-the-man-who-harmed-the-world-the-most

Gallo, C. (2016). *The storyteller's secret: From TED speakers to business legends, why some ideas catch on and others don't*. New York, NY: St. Martin's Griffin Press.

González, J., Barros-Loscertales, A., Pulvermüller, F., Meseguer, V., Sanjuán, A., Belloch, V., & Ávila, C. (2006). Reading cinnamon activates olfactory brain regions. *Neuroimage*, *32*(2), 906–912.

Heick, T. (2017, August 29). Helping students tell their story through social media. Retrieved from https://www.teachthought.com/technology/8-tips-for-helping-students-tell-their-own-story-in-a-social-media-world

Herreid, C. (Ed.). (2007). *Start with a story: The case study method of teaching college science*. Arlington, VA: NSTA Press.

Iwancio, P. (Producer). (2010). *7 elements in 4 minutes*. Retrieved from https://www.youtube.com/watch?v=NipDAd3_7Do

James, A. (2015, February 22). Persona 1 roundtable interview translated into English for first time. Retrieved from https://www.dualshockers.com/persona-1-roundtable-interview-translated-into-english-for-first-time-featuring-creator-scenario-writer-and-art-director

Kelleher, M. (2016, May 12). Beyond the DREAMers: Undocumented students tell complex stories. Retrieved from https://www.ewa.org/blog-educated-reporter/beyond-dreamers-undocumented-students-tell-complex-stories

Kristof, N. (2009, November 30). Nicholas Kristof's advice for saving the world. *Outside Magazine*. Retrieved from https://www.outsideonline.com/1909636/nicholas-kristofs-advice-saving-world

Kristof, N. (2012, January 21). How Mrs. Grady transformed Olly Neal. *New York Times*. Retrieved from http://www.nytimes.com/2012/01/22/opinion/sunday/kristof-how-mrs-grady-transformed-olly-neal.html?hp&_r=0

Lacey, S., Stilla, R., & Sathian, K. (2012). Metaphorically feeling: Comprehending textural metaphors activates somatosensory cortex. *Brain and Language, 120*(3), 416–421.

LaGarde, J. (2016, January 10). Stories connect us: 6 ways to empower your students to tell their own stories. #KidsDeserveIt. Retrieved from http://www.kidsdeserveit.com/single-post/2016/1/10/Stories-Connect-Us-6-Ways-To-Empower-Your-Students-To-Tell-Their-Own-Stories-KidsDeserveIt

Lang, J. (2012, September 20). Helping students to tell their stories. *The Chronicle of Higher Education*. Retrieved from https://www.chronicle.com/article/Helping-Students-to-Tell-Their/134502

Loehr, J. (2007). *The power of story: Change your story, change your destiny in business and in life*. New York, NY: Free Press.

Lucas, D. (2013, May 5). Raising the flag on Iwo Jima. Retrieved from http://www.famouspictures.org/raising-the-flag-on-iwo-jima

Mar, R. A. (2011). The neural bases of social cognition and story comprehension. *Annual Review of Psychology, 62*, 103–134.

Marek, K. (2011). *Organizational storytelling for librarians: Using stories for effective leadership*. Chicago, IL: American Library Association.

Marston, C. (2017, October 20). What "Professor Marston" misses about Wonder Woman's origins. *The Hollywood Reporter*. Retrieved from https://www.hollywoodreporter.com/heat-vision/what-professor-marston-misses-wonder-womans-origins-guest-column-1049868

McSpadden, K. (2015, May 14). You now have a shorter attention span than a goldfish. *Time*. Retrieved from http://time.com/3858309/attention-spans-goldfish

Meme. (2018). Retrieved from https://www.merriam-webster.com/dictionary/meme

Mock, G. (2011, October 14). Students tell their own stories. Retrieved from https://today.duke.edu/2011/10/studentbloggers

Morra, S. (2013). 8 steps to great digital storytelling. Retrieved from https://samanthamorra.com/2013/06/05/edudemic-article-on-digital-storytelling

Nix, E. (2014, July 1). The fascinating stories behind 8 famous photos. Retrieved from https://www.history.com/news/the-fascinating-stories-behind-8-famous-photos

Olson, R. (2009). *Don't be such a scientist: Talking substance in an age of style*. Washington, DC: Island Press.

Olson, R., Barton, D., & Palermo, B. (2013). *Connection: Hollywood storytelling meets critical thinking*. Los Angeles, CA: Prairie Starfish Productions.

Peterson, K. D. (2002). Positive or negative. *Journal of Staff Development, 23*(3), 10–15.

Peterson, K. D., & Deal, T. E. (1998, September). How leaders influence the culture of schools. Realizing a positive school climate. *Educational Leadership, 56*(1), 28–30. Retrieved from http://www.ascd.org/ASCD/pdf/journals/ed_lead/el199809_peterson.pdf

Robin, B. (2018a). Featured digital stories. Retrieved from https://digitalstorytelling.coe.uh.edu/example_stories.cfm

Robin, B. (2018b). The 7 elements of digital storytelling. Retrieved from https://digitalstorytelling.coe.uh.edu/page.cfm?id=27&cid=27&sublinkid=31

Ross, L. (2015, March 15). How to tell a story with your photos [Web log post]. Retrieved from http://lindsayrossblog.com/2015/03/how-to-tell-a-story-with-your-photos

Rowse, D. (2010). Telling stories with photos. Retrieved from https://digital-photography-school.com/telling-stories-with-photos

Shammas, B. (2018, February 23). Stoneman Douglas student journalists tell their own story after school shooting. *Miami New Times*. Retrieved from https://www.miaminewtimes.com/news/stoneman-douglas-student-journalists-tell-their-own-story-after-school-shooting-10115118

Silverman, L. (2006). *Wake me up when the data is over: How organizations use storytelling to drive results*. Hoboken, NJ: Wiley.

Simmons, A. (2006). *The story factor: Inspiration, influence, and persuasion through the art of storytelling*. New York, NY: Basic Books.

Stark, T. (2015). Crashing out with Sylvian: David Bowie, Carl Jung and the unconscious. In E. Deveroux, M. Power, & A. Dillane (Eds.), *David Bowie: Critical perspectives* (chapter 5). London, England: Routledge Press.

StoryCenter. (2018). Our story: How it all began. Retrieved from https://www.storycenter.org/press

Strauss, V. (2015, November 24). Teacher: A student told me I "couldn't understand because I was a white lady." Here's what I did then. *Washington Post*. Retrieved from https://www.washingtonpost.com/news/answer-sheet/wp/2015/11/24/teacher-a-student-told-me-i-couldnt-understand-because-i-was-a-white-lady-heres-what-i-did-then

Success stories: A tale of two schools. (2015). Retrieved from http://www.successforall.org/wp-content/uploads/2016/03/SFA_SuccessStories_Franklin.pdf

Valentine, D. (2010, July 13). A Yuji Naka interview—For the fans. Retrieved from https://web.archive.org/web/20160324211137/http://www.nightsintodreams.com/?p=1343

Wexler, A. (1996). *Mapping fate: A memoir of family, risk, and genetic research*. Berkeley, CA: University of California Press.

William M. Marston. (2018). Retrieved from https://discinsights.com/william-marston

Wilson, T. (2015). *Redirect: Changing the stories we live by*. New York, NY: Back Bay Books. (Note: The 2011 edition of this book was titled *Redirect: The surprising new science of psychological change*.)

Zak, P. J. (2014, October 28). Why your brain loves good storytelling. *Harvard Business Review*. Retrieved from https://hbr.org/2014/10/why-your-brain-loves-good-storytelling

Zak, P. J. (2015, January-February). Why inspiring stories make us react: The neuroscience of narrative. *Cerebrum*. Retrieved from http://www.ncbi.nlm.nih.gov/pmc/articles/PMC4445577

About the Author

Everyone starts with an origin story and collects tons of other stories along the way. Like many educators, **Mike Tveten** has followed a convoluted and meandering path, and the journey continues. After changing his mind about veterinary school, he ended up with a BS in wildlife science and an MS in entomology from Texas A&M University. Next came a half-hearted attempt at working on a PhD in entomology in Tucson, Arizona, which Mike gave up to take an insectary manager job at a "bug farm" that raised beneficial insects. (The only good part of the job was meeting Lisa, the office manager, whom he married.) Then there were temporary research jobs involving mosquitoes (ouch!) corn earworms, honeybees (worse ouch!), predatory insects in alfalfa fields, and looking at moth brains with a laser confocal microscope. At the same time, he taught part-time at Pima Community College, in Tucson. After four years as an adjunct teacher, it finally sank in that teaching was far more rewarding than research, and he landed a full-time job teaching biology at Pima College in 1992. Mike says it is now time to share the power of storytelling with other teachers, staff, and administrators.

Although Mike loves his job, everyone needs hobbies. Mike's include fly fishing, canoeing, hiking, and playing electric bass. Mike and Lisa spend summers in Montana in their 200-square-foot RV and the rest of the year in Tucson in their 400-square-foot tiny house. You can visit him at http://www.miketveten.com and http://www.imperativenarratives.com.

www.ingramcontent.com/pod-product-compliance
Lightning Source LLC
Chambersburg PA
CBHW020750230426
43665CB00009B/553